DEAR
WORLD

The Canadian Children's Project/Le Projet des Enfants Canadiens

CHER
MONDE

DEAR WORLD

The Canadian Children's Project/Le Projet des Enfants Canadiens

CHER MONDE

Les Enfants du Canada
The Children of Canada

Foreword by
The Right Honourable Jeanne Sauvé
Governor-General of Canada

Préface par
la Très Honorable Jeanne Sauvé
Gouverneur général du Canada

Conceived and directed by
Conçu et dirigé par
Ben Wicks

Methuen Publications/Sogides

on behalf of the Canadian publishing community
de la part de la communauté
canadienne de l'édition

Acknowledgements
Remerciements

CANADIAN CATALOGUING IN
PUBLICATION DATA

Main entry under title:
  Dear world = Cher monde

Test in English and French.
ISBN 0-458-80590-4

1. Social problems — Juvenile literature.
2. International relations — Juvenile
literature. 3. Children's writings, Canadian.
4. Children's art — Canada. I. Canadian
Children's Project Inc. II. Title: Cher
monde.

HN18.D42 1986   C86-094757-2E
            j909.82'8

DONNEES DE CATALOGAGE AVANT
PUBLICATION (CANADA)

Vedette principale au titre:
  Dear world = Cher monde

Textes en français et en anglais.
ISBN 0-458-80590-4

1. Problèmes sociaux — Ouvrages pour la
jeunesse. 2. Relations internationales —
Ouvrages pour la jeunesse. 3. Ecrits
d'enfants canadiens. 4. Arts enfantin —
Canada. I. Projet canadien des enfants inc.
II. Titre: Cher monde.

HN18.D42 1986   C86-094757-2F
            j909.82'8

Illustration en couverture:
Cover Illustration:
Kalla Haynes, 6, Toronto

Cover Photography:
Photographie en couverture:
Stewart Bailey

Book and Cover Design:
Design du livre et de la couverture:
Scott Richardson

"What would you do to put the
World right?" children across
Canada were asked. Their touch-
ing, often funny responses —
paintings, drawings, poems and
essays — are collected in DEAR
WORLD.

  DEAR WORLD is one of the
largest collective efforts ever
made to help the children of the
Third World. Publishers and
retailers have waived profits so
that all proceeds from sales can
be donated to the Wicks' charity,
Global Ed/Med Supplies, for the
establishment and stocking of
medical clinics in developing
countries. Many individuals and
major corporations worked
together to produce this book.
Special thanks are due to the
publishing and distribution staff
of Methuen Publications.

FREDERICK D. WARDLE
PUBLISHING CO-ORDINATOR

"Qu'est-ce que vous feriez pour
améliorer le monde entier?" On
a posé cette question aux enfants
à travers le Canada. Leurs ré-
ponses émouvantes et souvent
amusantes — des dessins, des
peintures, de la poésie et des
compositions — sont recueillies
dans CHER MONDE.

  CHER MONDE est un des
plus grands efforts collectifs
jamais faits pour aider les enfants
du Tiers-Monde. Les éditeurs et
les détaillants ont renoncé aux
profits afin que tous les produits
soient donnés à la charité des
Wicks, Global Ed/Med Supplies
pour l'établissement et l'appro-
visionnement des centres médico-
sociaux aux pays en voie de
développement. Plusieurs indi-
vidus et sociétés commerciaux
ont travaillé ensemble à pro-
duire ce livre. Notre gratitude
va à eux.

FREDERICK D. WARDLE
COORDINATEUR D'EDITION

Special thanks to the following for making The Canadian Children's Project a reality:

Nous remercions ceux sur la liste suivante pour avoir fait le Projet des Enfants Canadiens une réalité:

ADDISON-WESLEY PUBLISHERS LTD.
AIR CANADA
ASSOCIATION DES EDITEURS CANADIENS
THE BANK OF MONTREAL
THE BAY
DOUGLAS BEST
BOOKS IN CANADA
BRITTANIA
GEORGE BRYSON
CANADIAN BOOK PUBLISHERS COUNCIL
CANADIAN BOOKSELLERS ASSOCIATION
CANADIAN INTERNATIONAL DEVELOPMENT
  AGENCY
THE CARSWELL CO. LTD.
CELEBRATION STORES
CHATELAINE
COLES THE BOOK PEOPLE
DELTA HOTELS
T. EATON COMPANY
D. C. HEATH CANADA LTD.
TED HUGHES
ENROUTE MAGAZINE
GABOR COMMUNICATIONS
SHARON GOLDTHORPE
GOVERNMENT OF CANADA,
  DEPT. OF COMMUNICATIONS,
  THE HON. FLORA MCDONALD, MINISTER
GOVERNMENT OF CANADA,
  OFFICE OF THE MINISTER OF STATE FOR
  YOUTH,
  JEAN CHAREST, MINISTER
BILL HUSHION
PIERRE LESPERANCE
LITERARY GUILD
MACLEANS/L'ACTUALITE
MCDONALD'S RESTAURANTS
METHUEN PUBLICATIONS
DAVID MUNGOVAN
WM. B. PATTISON
PROVINCIAL MINISTERS OF EDUCATION
QUILL & QUIRE
READERS DIGEST
ROBINSON COMMUNICATIONS
ROBBIE ROSS
SCHOLASTIC-TAB PUBLICATIONS
SHOPPERS DRUG MART
SOCIETE DES EDITEURS DE MANUELS SCOLAIRES
SIMPSON'S
CLAUDE TAYLOR
TELEMEDIA — TV GUIDE
TIME
JOHN WELD
W. H. SMITH/CLASSICS BOOKSHOPS
WOODWARDS DEPARTMENT STORES

Judging of Entries

From the many thousands of entries received from Canadian school children, volunteers selected 400 for inclusion in this book. Thanks are due to that group and to the following who formed a panel to select the 30 entries judged most representative of the hopes and concerns expressed by all children.

Le jugement des concurrents

Des milliers de concurrents reçus des enfants canadiens, les volontaires en ont choisi 400 pour inclusion dans ce livre. Notre gratitude va à ce groupe et à ceux qui ont fait partie du jury pour choisir les 30 concurrents jugés les plus réprésentatifs des espoirs et des soucis exprimés par tous les enfants.

MARGARET ATWOOD
PIERRE BERTON
ROGER CARON
LASZLO GAL
MARGARET LAURENCE
MILA MULRONEY
MAUREEN MCTEER
KNOWLTON NASH
PIERRE TISSEYRE
DOREEN WICKS
BEN WICKS

Contents
Table des matières

vii   Foreword/Preface

x   Introduction

11   War/La guerre

25   Pollution/La pollution

33   Drugs and Alcohol/La drogue et l'alcool

37   Universal Problems and Everyday Concerns
Les problèmes universels et les inquiétudes quotidiennes

59   Hunger/La faim

69   Peace and Hope/La paix et l'espoir

Foreword
Preface

Her Excellency The Right Honourable Jeanne Sauvé
Governor General of Canada

L'Honourable Jeanne Sauvé
Gouverneur Général du Canada

In this era of international turmoil, the genius of youth is an inspiring tonic against the colder realities of our troubled world. Where too often we overlook the idealism of the heart in favour of more pragmatic factors, these drawings and messages are both a celebration of hope and a cry from the soul of a privileged generation puzzled by the cruelty and disparity of the world around them.

Above all, these young people remind us that this is indeed a "Dear World". We are made to recall that as custodians of this precious planet it is our inalienable duty to respect and conserve its valuable resources. Have we succeeded? The answer rebounds in the frank statements and subtle judgements of these children.

In this modern world of international communication, we cannot afford to dismiss the perspectives of youth as the naive ramblings of innocents. The mass media awakens our children at an early age to the more desperate conditions of the world around them, and then builds on that knowledge with every passing news report. Thus a ten year old speaks with authority on the dynamics of terrorism, a twelve year old on the crisis in the Middle East, and a four year old on the famine in Ethiopia. As the most informed generation of the modern world, these young people feel very much a part of the greater universe, in tune today with the international rhythms and events which will determine their future.

Dans un monde en proie aux bouleversements, l'enthousiasme de nos jeunes constitue un excellent tonique pour affronter les dures réalités d'une époque troublée. Si nous avons trop souvent tendance à oublier les idéaux de l'âme au profit des calculs de la raison, les dessins et les textes de cet ouvrage nous livrent un message d'espoir et le cri du coeur d'une génération privilégiée qui ne comprend pas la cruauté et les injustices qui s'étalent autour d'elle.

Par dessus tout, ces jeunes nous rappellent que nous devons chérir le monde où nous vivons et qu'en tant que gardiens de notre précieuse planète, nous avons l'obligation constante d'en respecter le caractère et d'en sauvegarder les ressources. Quant à savoir si nous nous sommes montrés à la hauteur de la tâche, les réflexions spontanées et les observations subtiles de ces enfants nous en disent long à cet égard.

En cette ère modern vouée aux communications internationales, nous ne pouvons nous permettre d'ignorer les points de vue des jeunes en les qualifiant de propos naïfs d'êtres innocents. Les mass média auront tôt fait de sensibiliser ceux-ci aux situations tragiques qui règnent de par le monde et continueront inlassablement de les porter à leur intention jour après jour. On ne s'étonnera pas dès lors d'entendre un gamin de dix ans parler avec assurance de la dynamique du terrorisme, une fillette de douze ans discourir sur la crise au moyen-orient ou un

If it is true, as William Wordsworth once observed, that the child is the father of the man, the value of these works is far greater than their immediate face value. They are a barometer of the future, reflecting with disarming clarity the values and aspirations of the society of tomorrow. As Canadians, the perspective of these children is influenced by the relative affluence and security of their environment. Whether this security finds expression in works of charity and caring or in terms of distrust and greed is clearly indicative of the future scenario of international relations and dialogue.

On balance, I would say from the indications here that the world will be in good hands. The spirit of love and fraternity, of good will and tolerance that emanates from the pens and crayons of these children bodes well for their faith in the ability of mankind to deal with the tremendous challenges before us. While all the solutions offered may not live in the realm of possibility, we are reminded that it is in the imagination where the greatest initiatives are born, and through the purest idealism that the impossible is turned into reality.

As Governor General of Canada, I am proud of the contribution of these young people. I congratulate them and all who have responded to this challenge to address our "Dear World" on their talent, their honesty and their desire to contribute their thoughts and ideas

bambin de quatre ans s'apitoyer sur le sort des victimes de la famine en éthiopie. Ces jeunes, qui représentent la génération la mieux informée du monde moderne, sont conscients de faire partie d'un plus vaste univers et demeurent attentifs aux tendances et aux événements internationaux qui détermineront leur avenir.

S'il est vrai, comme l'a fait observer William Wordsworth que l'enfant est le précurseur de l'homme, alors ces pages sont beaucoup plus révélatrices qu'elles n'apparaissent à première vue. Elles sont en quelque sorte un baromètre de l'avenir, évoquant avec une désarmante franchise les valeurs et les aspirations de la société de demain. Comme ces enfants sont Canadiens, leur mode de pensée est influencé par l'abondance et la sécurité relatives de leur milieu. Le fait que cette sécurité s'exprime par des gestes de compassion et d'affection ou au contraire par des sentiments de méfiance et de cupidité indique clairement la tournure que pourraient prendre les relations et le dialogue internationaux.

Tout bien pesé cependant, je crois que notre monde sera entre bonnes mains. Les sentiments d'amour et de fraternité, la bonne volonté et l'esprit de tolérance qui ont guidé la plume ou le crayon de ces enfants témoignent de leur confiance dans la capacité de l'humanité de relever les énormes défis qui l'attendent. Si toutes les solutions qu'ils proposent ne sont pas du domaine du possible, il ne faut

to the ongoing search for a resolution to the disparity and turmoil which exists around us. I am certain that those who read these messages will be greatly comforted and inspired by the outpouring of love and concern they contain. In that sense their very existence is a welcome balm to the pain and suffering of so many other children in this same dear world; it is a message that the goodwill of youth recognizes no political boundaries or territorial self-interests, and that the privileges and resources of this earth belong equally to all mankind.

pas oublier que de l'imagination sont nées des oeuvres admirables et que les idéaux les plus purs transforment le rêve en réalité.

En qualité de Gouverneur général du Canada, je suis fière de la contribution de ces jeunes. Je m'adresse à tous ceux qui ont répondu à cette invitation à montrer l'attachement que leur inspire leur ''Dear World'' pour les complimenter sur leur talent, leur honnêteté et leur désir de mettre leur imagination et leur générosité au service de notre quête perpétuelle d'un remède aux conflits et aux désordres que nous connaissons. Je suis persuadée que tous ceux qui liront ces pages seront réconfortés et inspirés par les trésors d'amour et de compassion qu'elles renferment. Leur message constitue en soi un baume aux misères et aux souffrances des nombreux autres enfants qui peuplent ce monde qui nous est cher. Il démontre que dans leur coeur, les jeunes ne reconnaissent aucune barrière politique ni aucune limite territoriale et qu'à leurs yeux, les beautés et les ressources de notre terre appartiennent à l'humanité toute entière.

JEANNE SAUVÉ

Introduction

Within the pages of this book you will find the dreams and wishes of the children of Canada.

They represent just a minute number of the thousands of our youth that donated their time in order to help the children of the developing world.

All proceeds from this book will be donated to Global Ed/ Med Supplies (Canada) Inc.

With the help of the Canadian International Development Agency (CIDA), GEMS will be providing primary health programs for the hundreds of thousands of children in the third world who are in desperate need. Progress resports on these centres and the life of the children living in the areas, will be relayed through the school system in order that Canada's children will be able to follow the progress of their commitment and by so doing, gather an insight into the lives of children living in other lands.

Without the help of many people this book would not have been possible. In particular we would like to thank the teachers of Canada. By their patience and generous giving of time they have once again helped expand the horizons of our children and taught them the meaning of caring.

Sur les pages de ce livre, on trouvera les rêves et les voeux des enfants du Canada.

Ceux-ci représentent une petite partie des milliers de jeunes qui ont fait don de leur temps pour aider les enfants des pays en voie de développement.

Tout profit de la vente de ce livre ira à *Global Ed/Med Supplies (Canada) Inc.* (GEMS).

Avec l'aide de l'Agence Canadienne de Développement International, GEMS fournira des programmes primaires de santé pour les centaines de milliers d'enfants au Tiers-Monde qui sont désespérément dans le besoin.

On dressera un état périodique de ces centres et de la vie des enfants qui demeurent en ces lieux par le système scolaire afin que les enfants du Canada puissent suivre les résultats de leurs contributions. Ainsi, cela leur permettra de comprendre la vie des enfants étrangers.

Sans l'aide de beaucoup de gens, ce livre n'aurait pas été possible. Notamment, nous voudrions remercier les enseignants du Canada. Par leur patience et leur donation généreuse de leur temps, ils ont aidé à ouvrir des horizons à nos enfants et leur ont montré la signification de la compassion humaine.

DOREEN WICKS.
EXECUTIVE DIRECTOR.
DIRECTRICE
GLOBAL ED/MED SUPPLIES (CANADA) INC.

War
La guerre

LEAH VOEGELI, 9, MAYMONT, SASK.

We were given the power and intelligence to make the world a better place to live and learn. Our intelligence has crossed paths with incompetence to produce highly intelligent machines for truly incompetent means.

There is nothing the world can do about this but hope that nobody is stupid enough to make everyone's most dreadful thought, a reality.

JEFF ANDERSON, GR. 11, MISSISSAUGA, ONT.

Dear World, how I would put the
  world right,
Without any bombs, without any
  fights.
Turn off the dark, turn on the light,
Split it all into equal rights.

If we keep fighting, life will be no
  more,
Why don't we just open up the
  door.
It's easy to stop, don't you see,
You're killing innocent people just
  like me.

RYAN MCLUCKIE, GR. 5,
LLOYDMINSTER, SASK.

11

If I was to make the bomb I would make it like this If some one made a bomb go off the only one killed would be he who set it off.

DENNIS SEMACK, 11, TEEPEE CREEK, ALTA.

PETER DUKE, 9, HALIFAX, N.S.

Le monde a besoin d'être changé
Si on veut que nos efants aient
    une bonne santé
On doit arrêter de tuer les
    animaux,
Sinon, les forêts seront remplies
    d'os.

On doit arrêter d'avoir la guerre,
Et on doit détruire les armes
    nucléaires.
On ne doit pas avoit des
    automibiliste ivres,
Si on veut que c'est sauf à vivre!

JONATHON JUCKER, GR. 5, TORONTO, ONT.

What I would do to change the world. I would dig up all bombs and disconnect them.

BRIAN HAYLEY, 9, BONAVISTA, NFLD.

If you look at the world
There is just no cease
To these endless wars
If we can't find our peace
It just goes to show you
That you can't have your way
If you don't really want to
Make others pay

You can build a shelter
But you just can't live in
Radiation will get to you
And you won't be 'llowed to win
S'go break your hearts
And break 'em all in pain
'Cause when it gets to you
It'll hit you like a train.

Poverty and famine
Are a real prob.
You really want to give
But you're too much of a snob
Doctor says they'll cure
But he knows that they can't cope
He makes a few donations
And he never gives up hope.

And I wonder if we'll ever
Make it 'till tomorrow.

REYAZ-ALIM KASSAMALI, 13,
VANCOUVER, B.C.

MARIANNE METEZ, 13, MEDICINE HAT, ALTA.

I hate wars that people start because they bother people. If the wars stop for about a month, say if I hired a man from the wars, and he said he wasn't in the wars, then later on he told me he was in the wars, I'd fire him.

JESSICA SKEAD, 8, McADAM, N.B.

Patrick D. Hutchinson, 9, Dartmouth, N.S.

All of your fighting,
All of your fears,
All of the wounds,
And all of the tears.
If all the people would look,
The people would see . . .
The world would be right,
With a lot more laughter,
And a lot less tears.

Kathleen Goodin, 11, Merritt, B.C.

The first and second World War; fighting of the nations
Was started by the older (bigger) generation.
These guys are just monkeys; They never have evolved.
They talk about their problems, But they never get them solved.
What are these monkeys called? Well, they're called adults!!

Michael Kim, 12, White Rock, B.C.

If I was in charge of the world for just one day, I would tell all the soldiers to put their guns and other weapons away.

If this happened all the soldiers would be free to do other work. Helping farmers who are unable to help themselves. Many farmers have had farm accidents, others are unable to pay labourers to help them with their farms.

Some rivers are polluted very badly because people use the river to dump their garbage. This could be removed with the help of soldiers.

Natasja Von Glahn, 10, Prince Albert, Sask.

Are you sleeping?
Can't you see
What's happening?
There is . . .
Noise and guns and . . .
and I'm scared . . .
Please don't fight.
Stop!!! . . . please

Cori Lausen, 15, Hanna, Alta.

We have to stop the bombs because they cause a mess. It could ruin the world really bad. Then people would have no homes. The bombs make a loud noise and kill people. Please stop. Please.

Clifford Rehm, 9, Teepee Creek, Alta.

I would like if there were no wars. and the world was more beautifuler.

David Kowalchuk, Gr. 1, River West Park

Mark Anthony, 11, Robert's Arm, Nfld.

13

ALAIN JOSEPH, 11, SYDNEY, N.S.

War can cause death. If all the people came to my house my mom would make them do the dishes and cut the grass. They wouldn't be any war any more because they would be too busy.

KIRSTEN HOPPE, 11, FULDA, SASK.

If I where a queen I'd get rid of war. I'd say: "No more weapons!" In wars people get Killed. Children lose their parents. When you fight with your sister, you don't use guns, swords, bombs, or canons. You use your bare hands. But in the war they think that they have to use weapons. Who ever thought of fighting to solve problems? To solve a problem they should talk it over not fight about it. The way I would stop it is to take 10 men of each country to play tug-o-war. The team that wins, wins the war.

JESSE ROY, 9, MONCTON, N.B.

The world is not a perfect place as you may know. If I had a chance to make this world right I would stop all wars to make peace possible. By destroying nuclear bombs. Why do people have wars. Can't we have peace? So many innocent people being killed. Little babies being killed moment after moment. Why? Why? Why? Because of greedy people who want everything. Power, Money everything,

In five years millions of people will be killed. Children won't live a long and happy life. We have at least a life of seventy years. We won't have a third of that if President Ronald Reagan and khadfy don't stop acting like childish babies, After all this is a matter of life and death for many people including me.

CATHY DANILEDIS, 11, MONTREAL, QUE.

The Wish
I walk through the field
which is thickly covered with blood,
I look for the dead and wounded,
who have all ran out of luck.

I see him lying there:

As I stand beside him in the field,
looking down on him quietly,
his aged hand moves towards mine
and his eyes slowly open.

My sweet little child, he said,
listen closely to what I say,
for in my life I have learned a little
and I will pass it on to you today.

Go and tell the world of peace,
of things they could do together.
Go set straight their poisoned minds,
so we can end rivalry forever.

Did you know that wars are awful
    times?
So many innocent people get killed.
The death, the pain, the innocence,
make sure it never happens again.

Those big, huge bombs still frighten
    me,
they make my hairs curl up.
Why would anyone want to destroy
    this beautiful world?
The creation of all God's love.

Now promise me before I go,
promise me you'll love
all the people in this world
who all deserve so much.

I nodded gently,
saying I would try.
But as I looked upon this man
his smiling face had died.

STEPHANIE FREY, REGINA, SASK.

DONNIE MACAULEY, MONCTON, N.B.

15

PAUL JUBENVILL, 12, WHITE ROCK, B.C.

If I were to put our small world right,
    I would try to do it overnight.

    First I'd end all violence and war,
    and to love and life I'd open the door.

    I'd stop whatever jeopardizes lives
    including weapons like eight inch knives.

    I'd do all I could and put up a fight, and that is how I would put the world right.

STEPHEN WILKS, TORONTO, ONT.

I am hear today to ask you why everyone insists on bombing and killing innocent people. Why can't everyone just for once be friends and not kill the person of he disagrees with him. Why can't we all live in peace and harmony for a change.

It would be great if we could accept people for what they are and be friendly with everyone.

PAM JONES, 12, REGINA, SASK.

There are many things wrong in this world. Such as wars there are at least fifty wars. Well, this is what I would do to make the world right. I would gather up all the Presidents and send them to another world where they could fight. All by themselves instead of distroing the world. Then one day I would go to visit them and see how they're doing if they're not fighting I would bring them back home and see how well they're doing. If they don't fight I won't bother them. But if they still continue to fight. I would send them back. Then this world would be perfect except for the bad guys. Well, I think I'll teach them a lesson that, they'll never do it again. This world will be so right that people would always leave there doors open when they go out.

MAMTA BHANDARI, 11, QUE.

16

As I lie on the cold, hard ground, I hear the sounds of gunfire, and people screaming, and can smell gunsmoke and blood. These belong under the heading, "war". I raise my head slowly, and look around. I am lying near the edge of a steep cliff. There are injured and dying people all around me. There are two soldiers far off to the left. I look at my clothes and arms. They are smothered with dry blood. I crawl towards the cliff, cautiously. I peek over, afraid at what I might see. What I see is too horrible to describe. I turn away, and in a daze see two soldiers throw another body off the cliff. His screams echo through my head. They come over towards me and pick me up. I scream!

This "dream" is not real and I didn't dream it at all. But I know that there are children that live in countries devastated by war who might have nightmares like this. If I could change you, World, I would have peace so no one would ever dream this.

CAROLINE BUTLER, 11, FREDERICTON, N.B.

Je vous demande si on peut arrêter les guerres dans les autres pays très comme l'Amérique du Sud là il y a beaucoup de chicanes et quelque fois des guerres. Si on avait des guerres dans notre province les choses serait tout en désorde.
Quand je regarde la télévision je pense à toutes les personnes qui sont mortes dans les guerres.

ERIN TRAIL, 9, MONCTON, N.B.

This is a beautiful country side.

This is after a nuclear war.

If I were the queen of the world I would take away all guns and knives. I would take away all bombs and other bad stuff, And then I would make sure nobody fighted by teaching them what war can do to them.

Also I'd take away cigarettes and cigars along with matches and liters so everybody would be safe and healthy, Also I'd take drugs, liquor, beer and wine away. So there will be peace and not as many wars and acidents, And everybody would be safe and healthy, And Happy

JANICE NG, 11, BEACONSFIELD, QUE.

If I could make a better world, I would invite the leaders of every country to come to Canada and sign an agreement that stated they would never fight again.

KAREN SUM, 12, DON MILLS, ONT.

Try to stop torture plesoe!

The world needs your help!

John Arnold, 8

Blayne Arseault, 12, Stoney Creek, Ont.

If I could rule this world, I would treat everyone the same, and if someone told a black person to get out of their house or store, I would have a long talk with him or her. I would have no wars and if two countries had a problem they could talk to me about it.

Andrea Moors, 10, Teepee Creek, Alta.

I would have a vote and all the people who vote to stop the world from fighting and those people will walk around the street with a sign saying "STOP THE WORLD FROM FIGHTING", and then I'll have another meeting and I will count and see how many more people agree. I'll start now 1, 2, 3, I will end up with 3200 people agreed to stop the fighting.

Trina Gaddes, Gr. 2, B.C.

There are no soldiers needed for this war cause one button will kill us all. So heed my warning, Dear World, For I shall tell you only once before the world self-destructs. From North and South, East and West we should all join hands in praise of life and dismantle all the nuclear missles, to make sure no one slips and ends our life with a "Boom".

Jason Bell, 16, Moncton, N.B.

I'm scared about the nuclear bombs between the "Super-powers". I just wish they would stop fighting and be friends. It's the same as fighting on the play-ground, only more serious. With fighting, nothing can be fixed. Please help me stop this nonsense!

Leanne Sargent, 12, Saskatoon, Sask.

Tania Ilic, Gr. 6, Brampton, Ont.

18

Since we are living in the nuclear age, making the world right would be a miracle. If I had to do it, I would start by getting rid of all the powerful weapons. The next thing I would do is get the world leaders together in a room. There would be a long table with chairs. Attached to the chairs would be everybodies name. On the table would be a pen and paper. They would write down what they would do to make the world right. After they finish, I would join all their ideas and turn them into one big idea. An idea that would make the world right. I would then give it to the world leaders and ask them if they liked it. If they did I would be very happy. If they didn't, then I would tell them to make an idea out of mine. If some of them liked it and some didn't and began to fight, I would have to lock them in until we finally get the world right.

ASHOK PATEL

A little voice asks,
   How . . .
I'd put the world right?
   Throw away all arms,
   Then . . .
No reason to fight.

A little voice asks,
   What . . .
Would I do as the leader of this
   nation?
   Everything possible
To save God's creation.

ANDREA BODDY, 11, ELLIOT LAKE, ONT.

NOELLE McBRIDE, 10, BRANTFORD, ONT.

How I would put the world right
Is take away all the fright
Of wars
And the worlds unfair chores

How I would put the world right
Is give everyone a silent night
Absolutly no crying
From babies who are dying.

NICOLE VAN DEN HOOGEN, 10, ANTIGONISH, N.S.

Dear World
I love you very much
I like living on you
You are very pretty.
How I would make you even prettier is if nobody living on you would be a litterbug. Just think why in the world would people put garbage cans on the street when people wouldn't use them.
O well it's been nice talking to you.
   Your Friend
   Angela Carter

ANGELA CARTER, 7, WINSLOE, P.E.I.

JOHN MORSTAD, 14, KELOWNA, B.C.

ROY BRYCE, 11, TEEPEE CREEK, ALTA.

We must have peace, unite our countries, let different races mingle and move to different countries and we should learn about different ways and customs also. In the near future this should prove to be quite useful. In this way the world could and should be "one big happy family." The reason I say this is because, just think if you were the leader of Russia and were planning an invasion of the U.S. of A. and just realized half of your population is over there having a good time for once. Well, that would surely stop you in your tracks.

CLINT MILLER, 11, GRANDE PRAIRIE, ALTA.

If I was the world I would be dizzy with confusion.
If I were the world I would be mad and sad all at the same time. Just think God gives people life, and what do they do but fight and kill one another.

TRACY JENNISSEN, 9,
CRANBERRY PORTAGE, MAN.

To Stop Wars I would say "Hi" to them and they would point their arrows the other way.

RYAN PEACOCK, 6 YRS 4 MTHS.,
TRENTON, ONT.

To make the world right I would
try and try and try my best to
put two enemies together. Those
are President Reagon and Kadafi.

Antonio Di Geronimo, Gr. 3,
Winnepeg, Man.

And then for the eagle and the
    great bear
Who've scattered their weapons
    over here and there
If they put all the money
They used for warheads
Into funds for the poor and those
    in hospital beds,
The world would be happier
And a better place to be
For the bear, the eagle,
    for you and for me.

North Darling, 13, Peace River, Alta.

I'd make everybody in the whole
world throw all the weapons into
a river, never to be seen again
and Everyone would become
friends.

Dawn Rehm, 11, Teepee Creek, Alta.

How I Would Fix The World
When We Have World War
    Three,
We should have it in Space
So on one on earth will get hurt.

Rob Miller, Gr. 2, Fort Sask, Alta.

Sean Keane, 12, North Vancouver, B.C.

To make the World a better place
I would make all the countries
lay down their weapons and
shake hands.

Robbie Healey, Kilbride, Nfld.

NUCULER
weapens
MAy they rust
in peace

Marco Barreiro, 11, Dartmouth, N.S.

To make the world a better place, I would take all violence away which would include - all South African battles, all attemps for World War III and any other types of violence.

DAWN MITRO, LONDON, ONT.

I would try to stop the wars in some places where wars are going on today. And some men just get killed fighting over money. Thats how they start a bad war. In some places where the queen lives there are wars going on there. And that is why she has soldiers and a very big house where she lives.

CRYSTAL PINEAU, 8, NORTH RUSTICO, P.E.I.

I would get rid of all the peple that make fights. That would make a good world and a good world is if no won would kill people and help the old peple.

MARK MACDONALD, 7,
CHARLOTTETOWN, P.E.I.

If I ran the world,
I would do away with nuclear weapons by taking them all apart, and that would save money to feed the starving people, then people could not have a war even by accident.

DIANA SHEPARD, ANCASTER, ONT.

DARCY LOGAN, GR 5, PRINCE GEORGE, B.C.

WADE SNOW, 11, ROBERT'S ARM NFLD.

Dear People Of The Earth,

If you were to stop this fighting and have peace on earth the would be no bang,
    clink,
    clang,
    boom
        the end.

From a concerned citizen.

STEPHEN BOUCHER, 14, MONCTON, N.B.

Leann Boyarski, 12, Medicine Hat, Alta.

I would put the
soldiers on farms
They grow crops.
The crops would
feed the
people.
The guns would
make good
fence posts.

Colin Mack, 7, Meota, Sask.

Pollution
La pollution

Text within the illustration:

DEAR WORLD, HOW I WOULD PUT THE WORLD RIGHT!!

Blue Skys
Blue Oceans
What a wonderful place to be
Please don't let the world end
Make it happy and free.

CHRISTINE BLAS, 10, DUNCUN, B.C.

"I would put the world right"
By trying hard with all my might
to stop pollution and hunger
But I have to stop and wonder
What the world would be like
Without troubles
Without Fears
Without Poverty and tears
the world's people could love
    each other
Mother, Father, Sister, and
    Brother

ERIN D. McRAE, 10, FAIRVALE, N.B.

I would make the trees sparkle in the sunlight and all the ponds tinkle a pretty tune. And make the flowers seem to smile when you look at them.

AMANDA LEWIS, 8, AGINCOURT, ONT.

Je vais mettre toutes les choses dans la poubelle oui oui. C'est bien.

NATALIE NOTT, GR. 2

ASHLEY MATSOMOTO, GR. 5

I would stop the people from polluting the lakes I still would like the world neat and tidy . . . and that people that pollute the water would quit right away so that other people can go swimming in the lakes with out swimming into coke cans and step on to glass

MATT ARDLEY, 7½, PETERBOROUGH, ONT.

C'est ton choix. Qeulque choses dans l'autre dessins sont un peu difficile a controller, mais le pollution pourait être controller, les feux, les accidents d'auto et les personnes sous.

Le monde en paix est un rêve qu'on peut réaliser!

SARAH DOBEC, TORONTO, ONT.

I will get all the pollution out of the air and the water. I would do that because I don't want the fish to die. I would get a long hose a bout 500,000 meters long. I would put the hose in space and I will take the uther end. I will take all the pollution and pumpit in to space. After I do that the world would be clean.

BRENT TOURANGEAU, 11,
FORT SMITH, N.W.T.

I would make poeple stop fighting by saying "If you fight anymore I'll kick you off the world if you don't stop fighting." But I really would not do it. I was just trying to make them stop. "If you don't stop the pollution you will have to clean the whole world. with a garbage bag." I think that would solve the problem.

PAMELA BLOOM, GR. 2,
JAMES THOMSON SCHOOL, B.C.

I should not bother the birds and
  the bees.
I should not damage Gods lovely
  trees.
wild flowers should be left alone.
nor should I write upon a stone.
All nature is a wonderful treasure.
God made it for His peoples
  pleasure.

RACHEL KIELSTRA AND JANELLE DE GROOT,
GR. 3, OKOTOKS AND CALGARY, ALTA.

NICOLE SPRINGER, 8, PRINCE ALBERT, SASK.

My first suggestion to make the world a better place would be to fight acid rain. Brian Mulroney and Ronald Reagan are trying to fight acid rain but they are so busy with free trade. A speacial groupe of people, that have nothing important to do should be assigned to clean up and fight acid rain. Three quaters of the people in the world don't know what thoes factories that cause acid rain make besides pollution. Maybe that way people won't buy products made by the factories. Or maybe the government will close the factories down, but that is wishful thinking! The closing of factories will cause unemployment but the cleaning up of acid rain, the replanting of forests and the restoration of wild life will cause more employment than the factories.

My second suggestion is to make a law against hunting animals. They are living creatures also. If it is necessary, then hunting can be permitted. But as a sport or for clothing, that is cruel. Trapping animals is worst. The animals is left dying a very slow and painful death until the trapper comes and kills it. So there should be a law against trapping too.

My third and final suggestion is to get rid of all nuclear weapons. Why do we need nuclear weapons? I hope there won't be a nuclear war. We are all human. If there is a nuclear war it would be a waste of time, since there would be no winner.

NICHOLAS TROTTIER, 12, BEACONSFIELD, QUE.

Si je vois quel-qu'un qui pollue je vais dire arrête. S'il n' arrête pas je vais dire: police police e't je vais dire que la personne pollue dans l'eau ou dans les égoûts.

AFIYA, GR. 2

I would push the earth in a good orbit so every where on the world would be perfectly habitable

CHRISTIAN MOUZARD, GR. 5, HULL, QUE.

I would clean all of the garbage up, tear down unsafe and unfit to live buildings and put up new ones where they are needed.

JOE SOETEMANS, 12, PARKHILL, ONT.

I'd divide the world in half and put all the the smokers, and armys, and puluters on one half and all the non-smokers, and kind, and non-puluters on the other half.

TIMOTHY LUCIER, GR. 4, QUEBEC CITY, P.Q.

DONALD GUY, 9, DUNHAM, P.Q.

JILL HORTON, 11, BRANDON, MAN.

Could there be a Spaceman from
beyond the stars?
  Maybe from Jupiter, Venus or
  Mars?
To meet a Spaceman would really
be nice,
  I'd show him from the Southpole
  to the Northern ice.

I hope he's intelligent and could
explain to me,
  Why our adults are polluting
  the sea.
And what about our hemisphere?
  And the change in the weather
  of our atmosphere?

I'd ask him to talk to our presidents
  And tell them about our earthly
  residents.
Tell them earthlings are just visitors
too
  That the earth belongs to the
  animals and children, too.

And that the wars and the
fighting is bringing despair
  Not only to man and the
  country, but now in the
  air.
Ask them who invented the
nuclear bomb?
  And who cares about the
  winners when the earth is
  gone?

Please, Mr. Spaceman, I'd say
with great trust
  What the earthlings are doing is
  greedful lust.
I'm just little now but not for long
  This is our earth where we all
  belong.

Could you, Mr. Spaceman, help
with all of this?
  I know our earth is really a
  mess.
But if you can, in your intelligent
way
  Teach us we're wrong and have
  begun to stray.

Maybe there's hope if You can
explain
  The reasons there's so much acid
  in the rain.
And why the air is filled with
unclean smog
  Also what is causing that blue-
  fumed fog.

Tell all this to our presidents
  Before back off to space you
  went
And maybe--- just maybe, they'll
all agree
  This earth will live long after
  you and me.

Bye, Mr. Spaceman. I know you've
done your best
  The earthling people must do
  all the rest.
I'll say, I'm so glad we had this talk
  Thanks for caring and the
  knowledge you brought.

Janice Yachimetz, Gr. 8,
Fort McMurray, Alta.

John Rantz, Don Mills, Ont.

Annie Demett, Quebec, P.Q.

je ne veux pas faire de la pollution et ne pas lancet de bom be atomique

Steven Oag, Gr. 2

Every plant and tree removed from the ground must be replaced with either a seed or another plant. There is to be no more littering. Instead of sending garbage that will decompose to the dump, use it on your gardens or bury it. I would like all schools to perform exchanges with other countries so they will learn about other cultures. Finally, teach your children at a young age things like honesty, kindness, lack of prejudice, equality, by setting examples. After all, they will rule the world next.

Stacey Edzerza, 13, Whitehorse, Yukon

JENNY LYNN BROHMAN, KITCHENER, ONT.

You'd have a big vacum cleaner that would suck up all the metal things around it at the bottom of the lake and then it would spit the water out.

TANIS ROBINSON, GR. 6

D is for *deer* growing in the forrest
E is for *earth* that is not poisoned
A is for *ants* which work hard
R is for *rivers* flowing with fish
W is for *worms* fertilizing the soil
O is *oceans* full of salt and fish
R is for *radio* which we listen to
L is for *land* which the farmers
   own
D is for *dogs* who chase cats

CHRISTOPHER O'BYRNE, 12, NIPAWIN, SASK.

BOBBY-JO HEKOB, 10, LACOMBE, ALTA.

Drugs and Alcohol
La drogue et l'alcool

I think that people stop robbing, mugging and killing. Sometimes when someone is mad they take it out on someone or something else. I think if someone is mad they wouldn't do anything that will hurt someone or something. I also think that people should stop taking **DRUGS**! Because when someone takes drugs they think it's cool, but it really isn't cool. They are only being bad to their bodies. I think that all of the cigarette companies should stop making **CIGARETTES**! because when the companies make cigarettes they think of it as making money, BUT if people would think of it before they buy a pack of cigarettes or take a puff to be cool they should think of what it is doing to their lungs. I also think people should stop all of the bombings and terrorisim. I think there should be peace.

ROBBIE VINEBERG, MONTREAL, QUE.

A child is coming home from a birthday party and is on a path. She meets up with a drunk and calls for her mother. A police man came and put the drunk in jail.

MARISA MABBITT, 9, FORT SMITH, N.W.T.

JEREMY FLEMING, GR. 6

Je n'aime pas les drogues. Je n'aime pas les personnes qui prennent les drogues. Mais j'aime les personnes qui disent non aux drogues!!

SUZANNE HENWOOD, 8, DIEPPE, N.B.

How Come

How come people drink and drive,
How come they swear,
and take drugs. It is all **SO**
DANGEROUS it makes me worried.
When you swear, drink or take drugs
it doesn't do a thing for you or us.
So PLEASE stop drinking,
stop swearing and stop
taking drugs.
It would
make the world a better and safer place for you and me so please STOP NOW.

HOW COME ???

Bonnie McMullen, Gr. 4, Calgary, Alta.

DON'T DRINK AND DRIVE

Lorenda Beuker, 9, Fulda, Sask.

First I would tell all the drug dealers to stop selling alcohol, whiskey, wine and beer and if anybody drank whisky or any of that other stuff, they would go into jail and be fed only good and nutritious foods and drinks.

I would tell all the hunters to only kill animals for food or else all their weapons would be taken away from them for the rest of their lives and they wouldn't get their money back.

I would tell the world that money isn't everything and that money is just pieces of paper with numbers on it. That's what money is.

Brandon Wilkinson, 9, Regina, Sask.

If I could fix the world I would stop all the drinking while driving. More than half of the people in Canada die because of drinking while driving and a quarter of those people are teenagers. To stop this crime I would turn into Super Drinker Stopper, I would sneak into liquor stores and quietly take the bottles and move them far away somewhere like the Pacific Ocean. Then there would more Canadians to live a longer life! Don't think you can go to the Pacific Ocean and find the bottles because I hid them in a special place!

Dana Flanagan, 10, Fort Smith, N.W.T.

Tell them to stop taking beers and drugs. I would help the poor people and give them money, food, and a house. Stop war-talk to them about it.

SHEILA KILABUK, 10, FROBISHER BAY, N.W.T.

People that drink and drive
always know when they arrive
People feel dandy
When they drink that brandy
When they get in their car
they don't go far
They drink and drink
but they won't be able to think
Then they will cry
when they start to die

DWAYNE WODNISKY, 11

The fourth thing I would change is having some place for winos to live. For example, in the winter I see winos sleeping under a bench or in wrecked cars even in torn buildings.

VIDAK CURIC, GR. 5, TORONTO, ONT.

TINA SCHMIDT, OLDS, ALTA.

CARMEN WILSON, 12, SASKATOON, SASK.

35

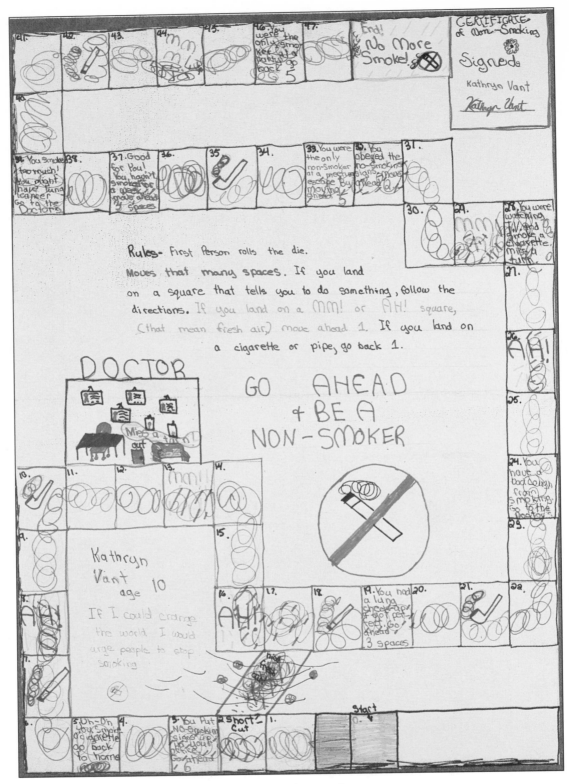

Rules- First Person rolls the die. Moves that many spaces. If you land on a square that tells you to do something, follow the directions. If you land on a MM! or AH! square, (that mean fresh air) move ahead 1. If you land on a cigarette or pipe, go back 1.

GO AHEAD & BE A NON-SMOKER

DOCTOR

Kathryn Vant age 10

If I could change the world I would urge people to stop smoking

Start

KATHRYN VANT, 10, OTTAWA, ONT.

Universal Problems and Everyday Concerns
Les problèmes universels et les inquietudes quotidiennes

If I could change the world I'd start with my own home. I'd clean my room and my brothers. Then I'd go on to school. I'll make sure there's only nice teachers like mine. I'd also check the children to see if they're behaving fine. If I could change the world I would start with little things because the world would change real fast this beautiful world of mine.

JANET THOMAS, 8, P.E.I.

If I was aloud to do something for the world. I would stop the people from fighting in the war. I would not allow smoking in the world. I would make sure everyone shares. I would make sure that the rich shared their wealth. I would give every animal a home.

BECKY JEAN BRUCE, 8, WEST ROYALTY, P.E.I.

If I were to put the world right I would help the people in South Africa. Just think you people about what you are doing, how you'd feel if it was you feeling all the pain being wipped to do work all your scars and bruzes no food these are South Africans. No water either they must feel sad the children oh what pain to go through the strain.

MARIKA BROWNE, 8, KITCHENER, ONT.

I would stop other people from ordering other people.

TAMMY GARPENTIER & LYNSEY JAMES, PETERBOROUGH, ONT.

I think it is wrong of people to be prejudice because no matter what colour you are, you are a person too.

LEANNE MICHELL BECHARD, 10, RICETON, SASK.

Let there be no time to sleep. All the people and me would not probably want mosquitoes. Let there be no jerks in the world.

EMILY KLASSEN, GR. 2, WINNIPEG, MAN.

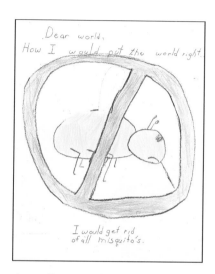

JUSTIN STRATTER, GR. 5, WINNIPEG, MAN.

JENNIFER LYNN POWELL, 6, BRANTFORD, ONT.

I would help Mom baby sit. I would change Tony's diapers. I'd sit beside Tony at the dinner table. If I don't sit beside him he will cry.

SANDY MOSS, CAMBRIDGE, ONT.

37

Robbie, 6

I WOULD MAKE OUR WORLD RIGHT, BY PUTTING OUR WORLD IN A......

....NON-SMOKING SECTION!!

Bobby Maxwell, Gr. 8, Toronto, Ont.

You ask me
How I would put the world
    right?
How I would make it
Peaceful, cheery, and bright?

I'd clean up the lakes
Move the factories away
So fish and plants could live
And children could laugh and
    play.

I'd stop the wars
All the murders and crimes
I'd stop the vandalism
And make the sun shine.

Everyone would be happy
Especially me
I would be proud
And I'd be filled with glee.

That's how I would put the
    world right
And I would do it with all my
    might.

Andrea Kirkman, 10

I wish there were no murderers in any city or town or country. Murderers are people that kill other people. I don't know why they become murderers. I don't know why some people kill other people.

One time in my town there was a murderer who killed someone who lived near the beach. The next morning the mother saw her dead and she started to cry. They didn't find the murderer. The mounties are bringing people in to find fingerprints.

We were all very sad. Some of the kids were scared at the school. It was not nice and very terrible. No one knows why it happened. Everyone wished that is hadn't happened.

Maybe if we give bad kids a little love and care they won't grow up to be a murderer.

Patrick Sageaktook, 9, Frobisher Bay, N.W.T.

38

If I could rule the world for a day I would buy a new car because my dad would like one.

Wesley Stevenson, 6, Victoria, B.C.

I would put the world right by putting on fireworks every night!

Tommy Welsh, Gr. 3, Pitt Meadows, B.C.

I would see that people weren't treated badly. I would make sure everyone had a friendly companion. I would give everybody a three week vacation to somewhere warm or somewhere cold.

Andre May, 11, Dartmouth, N.S.

Showing people how to farm, irrigate, write, read and survive on their own will help them live in a better, stronger country. It would also give governments in more prosperous countries more money to help the poor and unemployed. The way to do this is through proper management training.

Ian Robson, 13, Richmond Hill, Ont.

I feel that loneliness is one of the problems in the world. My solution would be to have every child adopt an alderly person. Then the elderly people wouldn't have to stay in nursing homes and institutions.

Monique La Pointe, 11, Winnipeg, Man.

I would stick up so many posters everywhere, saying STOP CRIME.

Marita Christie Borromeo, 11, Edmonton, Alta.

Today I woke up and said, WHOOPEE! It's My Day Today. I got dressed and found I had wings. I knew why. I was in charge of the world. I flew from country to country, with my list of things to do. This is what it looked like:
- help the homeless
- make evil not exist
- make love spread
- let sun and rain come as much as they want
- take all nueculear things (plus wartoys) away.

The list was much longer than that. By now I had finished all my deeds and I wondered what to do. I decided to have a world party. The question was: What kind of party? I decided on a mixed party. We had that party and we lived happily everafter.

Kerry Martin, 7, Victoria, B.C.

I would have a birthday party and invite all the people to come.

Robbie Lane, 6, Willowdale, Ont.

Rima Rowsell, 6, Hamilton, Ont.

Leigh Moore, 7, Seebe, Alta.

How I Would Put The World Right

They have the right to be free,
They need their own place to be,
Let the animals have the extra
space they need,
We don't have the right to take
their homes away,
They are God's creation and they
like to play,
They are Nature, so stop and
help them stay in our world.

Sandy Paddy
St. Theresa School Year 5

SANDY PADDY, 10, ST. CATHARINES, ONT.

Il fait plus d'argent.
HICHAM FARBAT, OTTAWA, ONT.

I'd make ice-cream, the national
   dish
And set bedtime hour whenever
   kids wish,
I'd make it so there is only 2
   hours of school,
Then get on our swimsuits and
   jump in the pool.
ROBYN SMITH, 10, NEPEAN, ONT.

I would make sure everyone was
treated equally. The native people of Canada would have more
right to make their own deci-
sions.
DAVID KOOP, 11, DWIGHT, ONT.

I'd like to teach
the world to be kind
it's a 1 2 3 4 everbody
stop fighting
and know
body is
poor.

MELANIE DOIRON, 9½, QUEBEC CITY, QUE.

JULIE O'BRIEN

I have a baby brother 5 months old, who can not hear and if I could make miracles happen I would cure that.

Sara Blum, 10

I would put the world right by having people work together. Just because you're a different colour doesn't mean you can't work with others. That's the greatest problem in South Africa. The Africans just can't stand it being put down by whites. All they want to do is be friends, work together, and share. The black children are fighting for freedom but they just end up dead. I feel terrible looking at the kids dead with their houses made out of cardboard. It's just terrible.

Stan Perentes, 9, Regina, Sask.

If I was in charge of the world for a day, I would make the whites in South Africa be good to the blacks. I would love to do this because I think that they treat them badly. For if you went to South Africa today you would see signs saying: No Blacks Allowed! or This Beach Is Reserved For Whites Only! They can't even sit on the same park bench. I really don't understand why the whites do this but if I were in charge of the world for a day, this would be the first thing I would do.

Angela Wiebe, 12, Nipawin, Sask.

Having not enough homes for everyone is not anyone's fault, except when we don't do anything about it.

Innes Pilatzke, 12, Nipawin, Sask.

I would get all the zoo keepers to let the animals free. I would stop war of any kind and I would put all cassinos out of business.

Steven Lloyd, Gr. 2, Prince Albert, Sask.

Personne ne mourrait de faim,
Tout le monde aurait du pain.
Il n'y aurait plus communisme,
Mais beaucoup de tourisme.

Aussi, pour améliorer la Terre,
Vous savez ce qu'il faut faire!
Personne ne serait sans travail,
Et on ne verrait plus de batailles.

Andrea Rabel, Gr. 5, Toronto, Ont.

On peut mettre sur la radio, on peut mettre sur la télévision qui dit arrete de faire les choses qui ne sont pas justes.

Jenny Razkumar, Gr. 2

I would give flowers to the people who are sad.

Jermaine Rover, 5, Willowdale, Ont.

Jennie, 10, N.S.

Kyle Izzard, 11

Tabitha, 5, Victoria, B.C.

Paul Hiatas, 11, Willowdale, Ont.

I would have a rule against parents battering their children. If I had the money, I would give it to the starving kids and parents in Ethiopia. I would have violence off of the television. I would have the war stopped.

Melissa Damboise, 9

I would make another planet in outer space and put all the people in the new world as I fix up the old one.

Eunice Kim, 10, Toronto, Ont.

This is how I would put the world right. There should be more fosterparents. Having more food banks and shelters for poor people. Convince people vandalism is not the solution. And also by burning war machines.

Jonanda J. Cuff, 10, Tsawwassen, B.C.

I had a chance,
To get better plants,
To stop nuclear power,
To get pure water,
To stop dictatorship and starvation,
And to prevent war and pollution:
I did it without hesitation.

I built a small city,
With trees numbered greatly;
In the middle of streets,
People found seats,
In a strange machine,
Which looked like a bean;
Industries, I did expel,
So pollution rate advantageously fell.

"No products that are chemical,
Only those that are natural."
Was one of the many rules,
Which laid punishment on some fools.
Nuclear power was replaced,
By the sun when it was faced,
And tempered in the night,
By the moon when bright.

The population of this little city,
Freely lived in amnesty,
War forever did cease,
Every human lived in peace.
No more cars on the street,
Gave people a chance to meet.
For all work, they would gather,
And share the joy altogether.

Once I had finished one city's birth,
I repeated this around the rest of the earth.
So I guess it must seem,
That this was my beautiful dream.

Karim's Kamani, 12, Toronto, Ont.

42

If I had the power to change the world I would give everyone the opportunity to live in a democratic country.

I used to live in a country run by communists and it wasn't very pleasant because they can push you around a lot and take your business away from you for no reason.

That country is Vietnam. In Vietnam we had a neighbour who informed on us even if we had chicken for dinner and my dad would get called to the police station to have a talk.

Vietnam had a money trade twice a year in which they made new money. No matter how much you turned in they gave you back $200.00.

In Vietnam you could do anything with money. Even if you killed someone you could buy your innocence with a bribe.

Finally my parents wanted to get away from there because we were almost broke. We knew we were doomed. So we left on a boat to Malachia and from there we flew to Canada. We couldn't believe we were in Canada. We were very glad but sometimes sad too because we left relatives in Vietnam.

So you see if it wasn't for communism we wouldn't have to leave our home.

KY AU, GR. 6, STONEY CREEK, ONT.

I would stop all the crime
In a matter of time.
Teach Africa to plant plants,
And give them shirts, socks and pants.

DARRYL ELLERT, 11, RICETON, SASK.

Protect Wildlife

NAILA ABDULAZIZ LALJI, EDMONTON, ALTA.

If I were to put the world right, I'd put my brother in jail (if he was being mean). There would be lemon-flavored medicine so you wouldn't have to get a shot at the doctors. I'd make my doctor Dr. Bowman give me more jellybeans. I'd make my dad, Dr. Paul Mitenko, take me to his office more often. I'd plant candy trees and you wouldn't get cavities from them. I'd make it that Grade 2's could be dismissed at 11:30.

SARAH MITENKO, GR. 2, WINNIPEG, MAN.

Stop killing whales.
Stop polluting. Listen to your father and mother. Stop hunting. Stop fighting. Stop killing people.
Start eating your dinner tobe healthy. Stop rabbing. Stop having Wars.

MARIE, GR. 2, QUEBEC CITY, QUE.

DEAR Right   how I Put the world

Love the people
who live in parks
and alleys.

GERALDINE SCHOLLAR, YELLOWKNIFE, N.W.T.

Upon this great world of ours
There has formed many new
*   powers.*
Each country tries to have its hold
On this strange prowess bright and
*   bold.*

Away from simple earthly
*   wonders*
We turn our heads t'wards these
*   thunders;*
Which echo with a dreaded
*   boom,*
And bring the toll of ghastly
*   doom.*

Away we look from the rainbow's
*   hue's*
Away from morning's glist'ning
*   dews,*
To turn and honor this cold idol
Binding with it's power's bridle,

Engulfing us in seas of a silence
Numbing our intuitive sense.
Deaf to all the cries of murder
Hearing only greed's faint
*   murmur,*

We close our ears to the hungry
*   pleas*
And friendships from across the
*   seas,*
Turning our backs on our dear
*   friends*
Is this how we shall meet our ends;

Away from those with so much
*   tó share*
Away from those 'bout whom
*   we care.*
With only the echoing boom
*   and our final dreaded doom?*

Yet if the veil could be thrust away
Letting in the light of new day,
We shall see the beauty again
And Glory in a fresh clean rain.

DIANE BOSMAN, 16, LETHBRIDGE, ALTA.

If I could change The world I would have no bad people and everyone rich!

MELISSA TREMBLAY, 10, AYLMER, QUE.

Queen For a Day

If I were in charge of the world,
I'd cancel swearing, smoking,
    drinking
and driving and also bad drugs.

If I were in charge of the world,
There'd be love, flowers and
    more rainbows.

If I were in charge of the world,
You wouldn't have rainy days,
You wouldn't have snowstorms.

If I were in charge of the world,
Candy would be good for you,
All cats would be dogs.

And a person who sometimes
    forgot to
flush the toilet and sometimes
    forgot to wash her face,
Would still be allowed to be in
    charge of the world.

AMANDA MARSHALL, GR. 1,
LARDER LAKE, ONT.

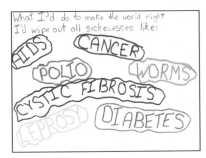

What I'd do to make the world right I'd wipe out all sickenesses like: AIDS CANCER POLIO WORMS CYSTIC FIBROSIS LEPROSY DIABETES

JAIME THIBEAU, GR. 4, MEAFORD, ONT.

MARIE GALLANT, MONCTON, N.B.

Dear World
I would save the endangered species around the world.

Africa   Australia   Canada

JESSE ESCH, 8, EDMONTON, ALTA.

I would make the sun shine all the time

KEVIN DUBECK, 5, WILLOWDALE, ONT.

How I would make the world right. I would find a cure for canser.

CHANI HONIG, DOWNSVIEW, ONT.

I would stop putting taxes on everything.

MICHELLE MERRILL, GR. 4, QUEBEC CITY, QUE.

If I were to make the world right it would be to make people not allergic to animals so they would have someone to come home to at night.

RENEE PROVENCHER

If I could change the world I would like to help the people who have cancer. Because it makes people very sick and my friend has it. And he has to have a needle in his leg.

LAURA JENNEX, 8, HALIFAX, N.S.

We have many problems,
both big and small,
but we swat them away,
like a fly on a wall.

We should stop for a minute,
and listen to the music,
and take our brain,
and try to use it.

CRAIG, TUOMI, 13, PRESCOTT, ONT.

I'd make the world right by making more room for wildlife and insects.

CINDY PURNOMO, GR. 5

If I could make the world a better place I would take away the cold North Winds so the sunshine would shine threw our hearts.

ANDREA FRANCQ, GR. 4, TIMMINS, ONT.

I would like to stop terrorism, high-jacking because I think that people are getting more frightened because they don't want to be kept hostage. They just want to be comfortable on anything and not to worry about getting highjacked, that's all. If they didn't agree I would offer them money food and house to start on.

CHRISTOPHER MUDRY, 10, EDMONTON, ALTA.

I would make a draw for a couple of poor people to visit me and other rich people will take two poor people every year, and treat them like a guest.

JENNIFER FORSYTHE, 11, BRUDERHEIM, ALTA.

46

Put wars to an end,
Make everyone have a friend,
Make people who need to eat,
Have some peas, potatoes and
 meat,
I would stop criminals that start
 crimes,
That steal our pennies dollars
 and dimes,
I would do all of this if I had to pay,
If I could just have the world for
 a day.

DAWN REES, 10, OLDS, ALTA.

I'd invite Bill Cosby to be the
President of the United States. I
think he'd be as popular with
Russians and Libians as he is
with North Americans. I'd ask
Bob Geldof to be President of
the United Nations. Mr. Geldof
recently raised over two hun-
dred million dollars. He brought
countries such as Russia and
U.S.A. together for two glorious
hours of jogging. I'd ask Mother
Theresa to become the head of
N.A.S.A I'm sure she would
immediately close it down and
redirect the money, scientists
and knowledge towards research-
ing medical and agricultural problems that affect the whole planet.

BECKY PACKER, 7, PEACE RIVER, ALTA.

You shouldn't watch violence on
television. It is not good for you.
Just say one day you were watch-
ing violence on television. You
can go crazy and hurt others or
yourself. I will not watch violence on television.

GINO GAGLIA, 8, MISSISSAUGA, ONT.

ISAK SARFATI, GR. 5

Regrettably, perhaps, the greatest problems faced by families of
handicapped children is lack of
understanding on the part of
uninformed persons, both adults
and children. I wish more people would inform themselves and
their children about giving con-
sideration to those of limited
ability. When parents do not
bother to explain the problems
of the handicapped to their children, difficulties often result.
There is just no answer when a
mentally handicapped child
climbs crying on his mother's
knee and wants to know, "What
does it mean to be retarded?"

JENNIFER RORKE, 13, UNITY, SASK.

All the young kids hanging
around would have something
better like a job or a bit of
ground. The kids would have
money, like adults do. They'd
have lots of money and pride
too.

ELISA SHAW, GR. 4, OTTAWA, ONT.

I would make it rain so flowers
will grow.

DANNY GREEN, 5, WILLOWDALE, ONT.

47

Poaching How would you feel if the animals started shooting humans? We wouldn't like it. So stop Poaching and treat wild life as you treat your children on friends

Respect Nature

KORY MULLIGAN, 10, KYLE, SASK.

Il faut des maisons comme les nôtres par tout dans le monde.

ADAM BROWN, OTTAWA, ONT.

If I could make the world right,
I would find a solution
To stop the polution
If I could make the world right.

If I could make the world right,
It would be like a symphony
Everyone living happily
Helping each other so lovingly
If I could make the world right.

If I could make the world right,
Everyone would be nice
To all the animals,
(Especially mice)
If I could make the world right.

ANDREW MILLER, 11, OTTAWA, ONT.

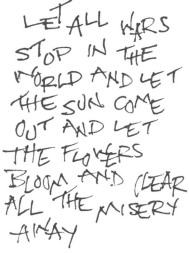

I think that there would be a Universal Housing Program (UHP). All the governments in the world should pitch in and build apartments, rest home and other housing possibilities. The (UHP) homes don't have to be royaly fancy but they shouldn't be covered in cobwebs either. I think there should be more houses than benches in 3rd world areas of the world.

DAVE MACKENZIE, 11, DELTA, B.C.

To make the world a better place,
A lot of things must be done,
Forbidding children to grow up,
is the most important one.

Do you really think we'd be in this mess,
if all children were in charge?
Would there be atomic bombs,
Mass murderers, or serious wars at large?

Most children are pretty sure of themselves,
though obviously some adults are not
Have I convinced you yet that children,
could improve the world a lot?

KRISTA WALSH, 12, ST. JOHN'S, NFLD.

LET ALL WARS STOP IN THE WORLD AND LET THE SUN COME OUT AND LET THE FLOWERS BLOOM AND CLEAR ALL THE MISERY AWAY

CAROLYN ANN CANNING, 9, BRACKLEY BEACH, P.E.I.

People should get same amount of money, and there will be no beggars.

KATHERINE CHAN

48

BEN ESCH, 6, EDMONTON, ALTA.

I would like it if they let all the imprisoned people out of Russia. All the poor will be comfortably rich and all the criminals set free because they have learned their lesson. If only people wouldn't be prejudice the world would be a better place.

It would be a better place if everybody would be kind to each other. The beautiful people be kind to the ugly people. The skinny people would be nice to the fat people. The world would be a better place if everybody were friends.

MIA QUINT, HAMPSTEAD, QUE.

I am writing you to give you some advice how to improve yourself.

The first tip I give you is to stop all terrorism. Stop all war before all mankind is killed. To make Russia a free land. Stop Syria and Iraq from clashing with Israel. To make peace.

Second comes the land. To make Ethiopia rich and fruitful. Stop the starvation. Millions of people are dying. We can't have that, can we? So stop it from happening!

The third is as follows: Some people are poor, some rich. Well I think all people should be equal. No rich, no poor, everyone the same. Don't you agree?

CARA MARSON, COTE ST. LUC, QUE.

If I were God
I would change hate and war to
    love,
Change guns to flowers,
Bombs to fruit.
Change enemies to friends,
Famine to feasts.
Change polution to a clean
    world,
Acid rain to clean rain.
Make a country for all bad
People
And get rid of all borders,
and make the world all one.
And I would stop people
from having the urge for drugs,
    or cigarettes.
But most of all
I would make people purple
So there would be no racism.

GARRETT HAMMER, 13, ST. LAMBERT, QUE.

Your World is shameful
Money is everything
Materialization is too much
Poverty lurks no money no
    anything
Except its own life

A part of me, an aching pain
    deep inside of me
Is crying out wanting to change
    everything
I see peace flowing through our
    leaders
Love and happiness
Nothing is dead except war

JENNIFER C. EDWARDS, 13, GRAND FALLS, NFLD.

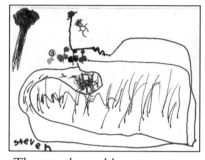

The people could come to see me and see all my flowers.

STEVEN MEYFROOT, 6

I don't like people killing animals.

WESLEY HATANO, GR. 2, CALGARY, ALTA.

49

If I could put the world right I would put two water-slides in each town and city in Canada, I would get rid of all the insects, I would make school start in October and end in February. I would make the movie fifty cents to get in and popcorn fifty cents too, and make everything cost under twenty dollars. I would make the beach water warm by putting heaters in the water. At the swimming pool there would be lots of wet slides. I would put McDonalds, Dairy Queen, and Burger King up town.

DEBBIE PIEPER, 11, YELLOWKNIFE, N.W.T.

JIA MIN, 7, SCARBOROUGH, ONT.

I would change the wrongs to
  rights
By stopping all crimes and stop-
  ping all fights
I would make sure that after
  hours in a bar
We don't come out and drive in
  a car
There has to be a good solution
To stop a terrible thing called
  pollution
I would try to help starving
  people too
But that's one thing we've al-
  ready started to do
Now I would just have to keep
  some important things
Like summers, winters, falls and
  springs
I would have to keep the air and
  care
Those two things are very rare
So the world is really not that
  bad a place
Bud I'd change some things just
  in case!

KELLY BROWNE, GR. 5, OSHAWA, ONT.

I'd give some homes to people who
  care
and people who are poor would be
  treated fair.

People would be taken care of and
animals are treated with care.

But since I can't change the world
  I'll just share.

CHRISTINE O'NEILL, 12, FREDERICTON, N.B.

J'aimerais que tous les autres pays et le Canada soient propres, passales.

Derek Brez, Ottawa, Ont.

I would put the people in Africa on a plane and take them to Canada.

Rebecca Bilodeau, 8, Dartmouth, N.S.

As you probably know, this world is filled with bad things and me, Jennifer Li is going to solve that. You see, that if you take out all the bad people and let the good people stay in, that would be perfect; but how would I do that. Ummm. . . . Mabey I can invent something. If I take a brisk walk down the street it might clear my mind. Opps, my key fell in that hole. I can't reach it, here it is. No that is not it, its just an old glass ball. (So I shot over my shoulder and crash! I turned around it was broken.) Then a cloud of smoke appeared and some sort of elf came out. ''I will grant you two wishes because you freed me from that old crystal ball.'' The elf shouted to me but I was thinking of the two wishes so I said. ''But about the two wishes, I would like to have all the bad out of where they are and . . . . . Poof!! All the bad people were in and around my house and there were punks and there were knives and robbers with there guns I was horrified. So I yelled to the elf. ''Let these people back where they come from!'' Then Poof!! They were all gone then the elf disappeared too, so I said ''Well, you can't win them all.''

Jennifer Li Pool Than, 11, Montreal, Que.

I would not allow any presidents, queens or prime-ministers. Then we would not have any trouble.

We could save up lots of money and give it to the National Capital Commission and they would make the world clean and sparkling.

Stephanie Longpre, 9

I would make the sun shine so that the flowers and vegetables and grass would grow.

Keith Strain, 6, Willowdale, Ont.

I would change so I'm not thinking of myself. Not one bit!

Susan Vandermeer, Gr. 2, Calgary, Alta.

51

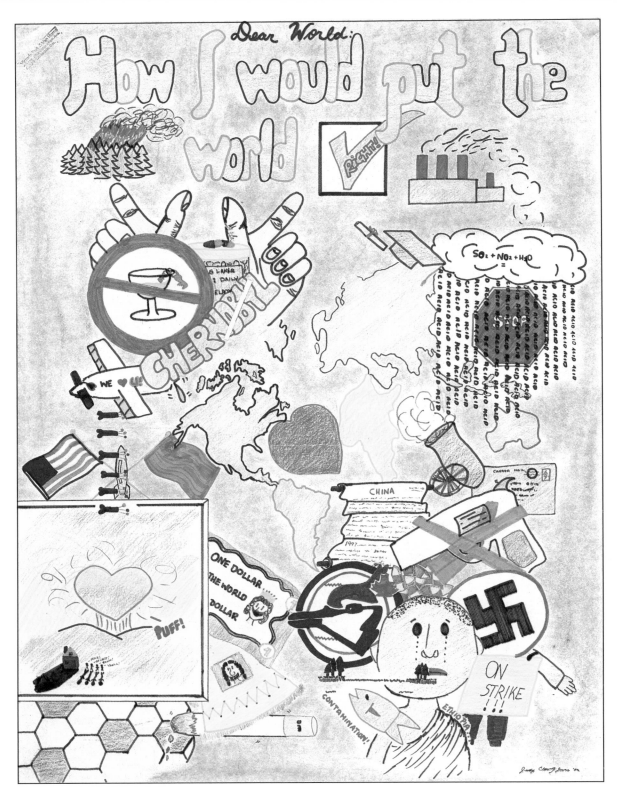

JUDY CHEUNG, GR. 7, SCARBOROUGH, ONT.

I would not let the men kill
Elephants for their ivory tusks
because they are very rare
and atractive to alot of people.

Jaime Thibeau, Gr. 4, Meaford, Ont.

One day, I received a phone call from the Prime Minister of Canada. He told me that tomorrow I was going to be ruler of the world. Boy, was I excited. Mr. Mulroney told me that this extremely important job was only for a day. My Plane for Ottawa leaves at 6:00 a.m.

(At Ottawa.) When I stepped off the plane, a whole gigantic crowd of people cheered. Gee, I thought I feel like a star! Hold on stupid, I thought again, I was ruler of the world. Mr. Mulroney led me to a door marked "Nobody but VIP's in here. Mr. M. introduced me to everyone there including Queen Elizabeth II and Ronald Reagen! "I'm planning to make a couple of changes. Number 1, I would like to send lots of food to poor countries like Ethiopia. Men! Fill up 30 truckloads full of food and then fly it to Africa. Get it! Good!" (By that time I was all ready to give orders.) "Number 2, I would also like the third-world people to be examined by doctors, Mr. M?" "Yes, I'll contact them right away." Mr. M. obediently said. Next thing is that I would like to employ some unemployed people. Speaking of jobs, all wages from doctors to secretaries should be about the same. It would be so much nicer and I don't think very many people would blabber on and on about their fancy homes and furniture.

At 7:30 pm I packed and then I was in a limo going to the airport. It was a day I wasn't going to forget.

Karen Lu, Gr. 5, Dawson Creek, B.C.

I would tell everybody no killing and no fighting and no robbing. At all the schools I would insist on no snowball fighting. And all adults must not smoke. It is bad for their lungs. All the shows on t.v. must be good for children of all ages. All the big kids must not pick on the smaller ones. If they did they'd get banished for the rest of the month and if they really hurt the little ones, they would be punished for two months.

And no saying bad words like the F word.

Angela Sorfleet, 9

Then I would make a day be Missing Children Day. All stores and businesses will close and everybody will go out looking for missing children. Whoever finds a missing child gets a free meal at McDonald's.

Jason van Mulligen, 11, Brandon, Man.

Il faut encourager
les recherches
en médecine.

Andrea Rambeau

Dear world
How I would put the world right!
I would Plant trees to give eveyone lot's of Shade

Lenny Faustino, Gr. 1, Woodbridge, Ont.

53

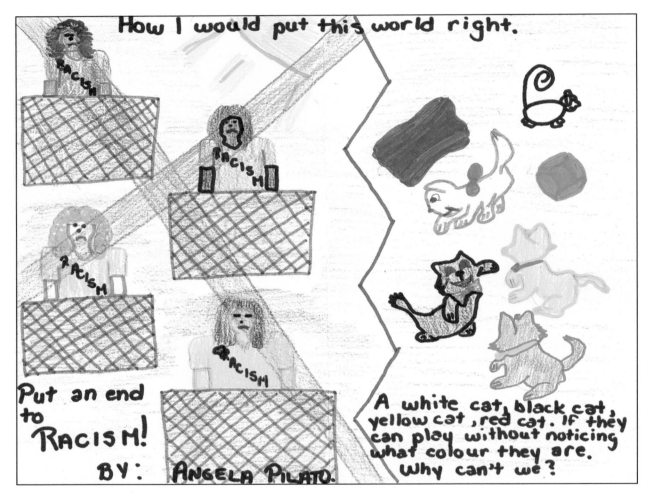

ANGELA PILATO, 13, DOWNSVIEW, ONT.

The rich would not be able to tear at the hearts of the poor anymore for the poor will store all the love they receive and always have room for more.

We all have chores to make the world a honorable home.

JULIE SHARPE, NACKAWIC, N.B.

If the boys and girls that were on earth had eaten a bad pill bad things wouldn't happen. Like dogs wouldn't have rabbies and people wouldn't have big rashes on their back.

MARY GAINNIS, 7

Je vais prendre les animanx et les mettreau Zoo, pour qu'ils manquent de rien.

MEGHAN MYLES, OTTAWA, ONT.

I'd lower the prices of important foods like milk, bread and meats and I would make liver unedible.

JONATHAN BUCHAN, 11, YELLOWKNIFE, N.W.T.

I'd send up a plane that carried a sign that said STOP ALL TERRIBLE THINGS. That's what I'd do.

SEAN MINAKER, 8, VICTORIA, B.C.

The world's changing day by day. Some days are good, some are bad. People work, people don't. Towns, cities are starving. I just don't know how to put the World right.

DEBBIE NEIDER, 16, PINE POINT, N.W.T.

Do not push in the hall. Don't fight with your sister at home.

RAYMOND LEE, 7

I would stop my mum and dad shouting at each other all the time.

ANON., 6, B.C.

55

Erin Freeland-Ballantyne, 4½,
Yellowknife, N.W.T.

"A Talking Wolf?" I said to myself last week while brushing my teeth. My little sister said "It's a hungry beach ball." "There it goes again!" I yelled. I couldn't stand it! I had to grab my flashlight and investigate! I took my 5 week old flashlight, slipped into my coat and ran outside. The talking wolf turned out to be a poor religious man looking for food! Well, he was taken care of. I called up my fourth cousin Irvine, and we organized a club for poor people with the government. Boy, what a busy week it was, calling up people and asking them questions.

David Oppenheim, Montreal, Que.

I would make a rule that no fighting between Girls or boys. No riding through the wilderness with dirt bikes and no shooting animals.

Allison Meier, 7, Kelowna, B.C.

I would probably tell the principal to tell the teachers to not give homework because we work 8 hours a day and I think that is a lot. I would also invent new sports and new games and new toys. I would make money fall from the sky instead of rain I would also make homes for the homeless people and give them some money to live. I would hope that crossing gards would stand on all the busy streets so not another kid dies. Most important I hope for no war.

Jason Hechd, Cote St. Luc, Que.

Joshua Keigan

I would help the needy by putting an add in the newspaper and ask people for money. At least 5,00$. And then I would get medicine for those who have a disease. Then food, shelter, and gardner tools.

Erica Jacques, 11, Beaconsfield, Que.

There are many things I'm sure this earth could do to become a better and safer place to live. One of these is getting rid of racism.

Racism is the worst feeling you can have. It's kind of sad though, because everybody feels racism at something or someone at one point. Some people dislike others because of the colour of the skin. There is a simple explanation for different colours of skin. The skin colour is determined by the amounts of certain chemicals it contains. These chemicals are called melanin and carotene, or pigments. Melanin gives the skin its brown-black colour and the carotene gives the skin yellowish tones. The pink in your skin comes from all the capillaries near the surface. Everybody has different amounts of these chemicals. Different skin colour is just like different coloured hair and eyes. There is no reason to dislike anybody because of skin colour.

I think there should be equal treatment between people of different cultures because everybody has a culture. I think my culture, the Chinese, is very rich and colourful. The world has a rainbow of cultures and mine is one of them. I don't see why anybody would want to "pick on" one particular culture because of languages, features or actions.

When we play it is nice to play nicely.   Spencer Day.

SPENCER, 6, VICTORIA, B.C.

Religion is just something you believe in. It doesn't matter what religion you are. You are still a human. It's like if one person idolizes a T.V. star and you idolize another. Does that make a difference. No! It shouldn't!

Notice that all of the people I have mentioned have two eyes, two ears, one nose, one mouth, one body, two arms, two legs, two hands, two feet, and ten toes and fingers—unless there was an accident. Everybody is a human being! It doesn't matter if their skin is a different colour, if they are of a different culture, or if they are a different religion. We are ALL humans!

ELAINE YONG, 11, REGINA, SASK.

Erin Kreutzwiser, 8,
Milton, Ont.

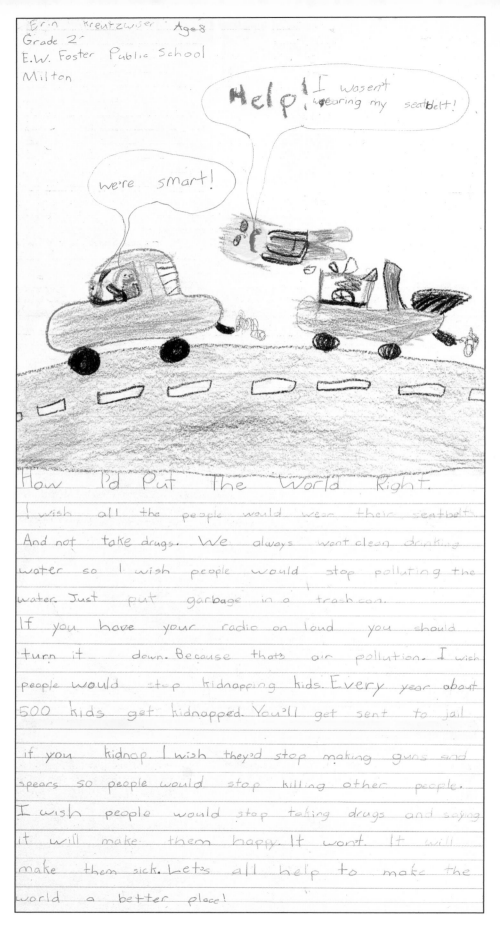

How I'd Put The World Right.

I wish all the people would wear their seatbelts. And not take drugs. We always want clean drinking water so I wish people would stop polluting the water. Just put garbage in a trashcan.

If you have your radio on loud you should turn it down. Because thats air pollution. I wish people would stop kidnapping kids. Every year about 500 kids get kidnapped. You'll get sent to jail if you kidnap. I wish they'd stop making guns and spears so people would stop killing other people. I wish people would stop taking drugs and saying it will make them happy. It wont. It will make them sick. Let's all help to make the world a better place!

Hunger
La faim

I would ask every one to adopt a Ethiopean child to give love and food to keep warm and alive.

<small>KELLIE LAIRD, 7, VICTORIA, B.C.</small>

If I could make the world right I would give food and water to the people that are starving. To stop the wars I would build a big wall in between the people that are fighting.

<small>HEATH DREGER, 9, EBENEZER, SASK.</small>

It seems there are three kinds of people, the ones that have everything, the ones that live well and the ones that have nothing. There are rich people that give millions to buy food for the needy, but there are more who keep everything to themselves and don't care about anyone else.

Some people sit in big mansions with a feast before them, hoping to make a profit in the stocks they just bought while others lay on the dirt floor of their tent, hunger gnawing at their stomachs hoping their child lives till the next food ration comes in by plane.

<small>JEFF HARRIS, 12, B.C.</small>

<small>SHANE O'BRIEN, 15</small>

JENNIFER WILSON

I have a little friend in africa
she is poor but she wrote me
a letter she has a sister and
brother. She is our new foster child.

LILLI AHRENS, 8, PETERBOROUGH, ONT.

CORRIE CASSALMAN

We have to give food to other countries. If we don't there will not be any people in some countries, and we need other countries you know. So we will have to teach them how to irrigate and how to plant food, and we will give the materials to do this.

And how about the people without an Education? Everybody needs an Education, or how will they know the best ways to grow food and crops and how to divide land and goods equally.

ROBBIE ANDERSON, 8,
SHERWOOD PARK, ALTA.

*I would let the people have all the
    food,
As long as it was nutritious and
    good.*

*The people could do whatever they
    please,
And get paid 10¢ whenever they
    sneeze.*

*They could have ice-cream sundaes,
On Sunday and even on Monday.*

*The day would end very soon.
So I would give everyone a present
    of one raccoon.*

*That would end my day, so into
    bed,
And not another word said.*

The End

SARAH MACKAY, GR. 4

Compare the amount of food we throw out daily, to the amount of people dying of starvation in the Third World. Or the amount of unnecessary food we eat compared to the amount of people lined up at food banks or picking garbage just to get a bite to eat?

JENNIFER FEHRENBACH, 14, DEEP RIVER, ONT.

I'd show people how to share, love and care for each other, especially the ones that needed it the most, like the little starving and ill children in Africa.

SIGRUN GULDEN, 11, WESTBOURNE, MAN.

Je dirais auxpersonnes de donner do la nourriture, des graines pour les jardins et des outils afin d'aider les pauvres en afrique.

AMANDA HARWOOD, 7, MONCTON, N.B.

The Third World is in need,
You should hear their shouts of
  plead,
There's a great lack of food,
And many children must go nude,
Everyday some children die,
Don't feel sorry and just sigh,
They need more & more supplies,
So don't just sit back and ask why?

GARRY HEINTZ, LLOYDMINSTER, ALTA.

Blueberry trees all over the world would be nice, because people could pick the berries and eat them.
JULIE SERRAO, 5, DOWNSVIEW, ONT.

JANICE GROVEN, 10, OLDS, ALTA.

HEATHER BEST, GR. 5

MATTHEW LORDLY, 12, HALIFAX, N.S.

Dear world,
I wold like to send lots of food to you.
I want to see you healthy and strong
I will send clos to the
salvashin ARMy to the world
Your friend
Ricky

RICKY FRONTE, 8, SCARBOROUGH, ONT.

If they're were not any poor or starving kids I would like to have a candy world but there is people that need help so I think I'd help everyone of them.

MELLISSA DOUCETTE, 8

When I go to sleep at night, I'm not worried about where my next meal will come from, or if I will even have one. Some people, in third world countries and in Canada, do. They fight for life and if they are lucky they find something to eat.

JUANITA MacNEIL, 15, PINE POINT, N.W.T.

Oh how could I put the world right?
I think it could happen in one day
  or night,
Look at the tears in faces
  everywhere,
We should help them and show
  them we care,
Why do we make bombs and guns?
When we could be feeding the
  hungry ones.

DORIS HAUSLEITNER, 11,
WHITEHORSE, YUKON

Pour aider Les enfants dans l'Afrique ils n'ont pas demanger. Les enfants dans l'Afrique sont pauvres. Je veux donner de la nourriture.

RUDY MacNEIL

I would make sure that at thanks giving everyone would get a turkey with gravy and a pumpkin to make a pie with or else it would not be fair.

LINDSAY TURNER

I would stop people from starving by giving them food. I would sow fruits and vegetables and I would make bread and cookies for them.

I will make sure that they learn to read.

If people learn to read they may be able to get a job.

WANDA JACOBS, 11, WESTPORT, NFLD.

SOPHIA STEWART, OTTAWA

I would give food to the poor and I would stop wars.

I would give homes to the people who need places to live.

I would put rainbows in the sky and that will make lots of love. It is pretty to have colours in the sky. I would plant flowers, trees, grass and food.

LYNN LEE

*If I controlled the world a day,
I'd stand upon a stool and say;
"Since now is my day in control,
I'd like you all to do your role.
To help the starved in other places,
who cannot find their lucky aces.
All I ask for you to do,
is give us something to them from
    you."*

CATHERINE DONKIN, 11,
GRANDE PRAIRIE, ALTA.

JUSTIN MICHAEL CLAUDE, 7, SASKATOON,
SASK.

63

JASMINE BIERLE, GR. 5, DELTA, B.C.

MELISSA DENNY

If I can see in
a starving child's eyes,
the truth.
That we should all share
and work together
then why can't you?
We all live
in the same world.

SHARON BROMWELL, 16,
WHITEHORSE, YUKON

I would want peace and friendship and let everybody have food so no one would starve. I would want the scenery to be pretty and more trees in the forest. I would like a hospital with lots of machines to help people. I would want someone to stop all the wars. I would want no more drugs and no more alcohol for the kids.

CHRIS SHECK, 11, YELLOWKNIFE, N.W.T.

There will be no violince on television there will be only cartoons. And also there will be no drugs and no polution and big stormes. It would rain in Africa and food would grow and people would stop spending money on weapons. And life and the earth will be just like a paradise.

KIM SAVARD, Quebec

I would ship food to the hungry and I would ask authors and actors to translate their shows and books into different languages. Then I would make rain where crops were dying. Then I would make astronomy easier. Then I would make no mosquitos!!

ROBERT JASON PITTMAN, 10, YELLOWKNIFE, N.W.T.

I would clean this world But there are millions of People who are dying and they have flies on them. I would give them food.

SANDY MONAGHAN, 6, PETERBOROUGH, ONT.

CHAD BRYDEN, 10, SYDNEY, N.S.

Je vais planter des légumes

CHRISTINA BROAD

Darryl Gauthier, 9, North Rustico, P.E.I.

Graham Wilson, 10, Lacombe, Alta.

James Tod, Ottawa

Une personne a pris une pomme pour une pauvre personne

Lucas Anderson

War is nothing to sing about
Or to be dancing with glee,
People are starving throughout the
    world
So help them if you agree.

If this was really up to me,
I know what I would do,
Donate to the poor and also the
    starving
So you all might do it too.

Andrea Oh, 11, Whitehorse, Yukon

I'd make all important things like food free.

Darcy Logan, Gr. 5, Prince George, B.C.

If I were Queen for a Day I would Stop Fighting with the poor-people. And give them some money.

Suzanne Hines, 7, Dartmouth, N.S.

If I controlled the world,
All the children would stand up.
No one would be hungry.
No one would be naked.
For once, everyone would be equal
And the circle of children perfect.

Donna Bell, 13, Morden, Man.

There are children who live far
    far away.
Who go to bed hungry every
    single day.
I wish I can help them and I'm
    ready to pay.
I'll give a dollar and show them
    the way.

Yehyda Zolty, 7

I would make the world right by giving better education to the people who need it, help prevent suicide by giving more love.

Chris D. Bradley, 9, Tsawwassen, B.C.

Trixie Blake, 14, Westport, Nfld.

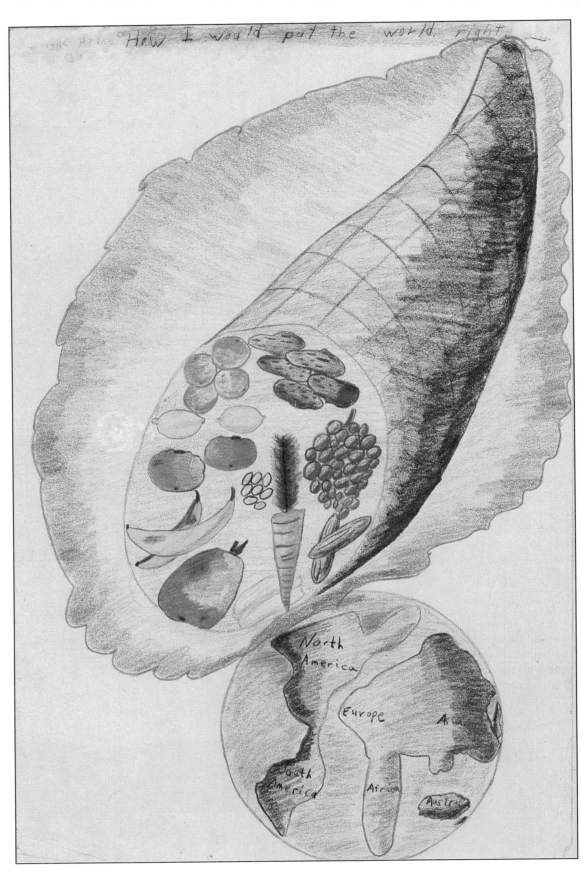

PARRISH SHERRARD, 8, NEWCASTLE, N.B.

Peace and Hope
La paix et l'espoir

The world would be a better
  place
if everything was not a race.
"I want this
You want that
I am beautiful
You are fat."
It's one big fight
Day and night.
This is no good.
This will not do.
The change must come
in me and you.

MARY ANN BARKER, 11,
GRAND FALLS, NFLD.

Mon monde est une très bonne
  place
Et nous pouvons nettoyer
Il ne va pas en avoir de guerre
Les animaux va viure en Paix
Les personnes peuvent aider les
  autres
Et pas de pollution
Un meilleur monde va être bon
Ronde et ronde va le monde

Mon monde est bon
Ouest, Est, Nord, est Sud
Ne conduis pas d'Autos
Des personnes doivent manger
  est travailler
Et ça va être un meilleur monde

CANDACE TRENTON, 10, ACTON, ONT.

I would want to teach
people about God's love
so there could be peace and
less greed and selfishness—
people need to care and respect one
  another
more, and there would be less war.

LORI BROOKES, 9, TSAWWASSEN, B.C.

ALLI MARSHALL, 10, YELLOWKNIFE, N.W.T.

**I'd like to make a happier world
by donating my love to others.**

SHANNON BROWN, GR. 3, PITT MEADOWS,
B.C.

To a Dear Parent

Help me to understand this
strange and complicated world
of ours. Give me enough freedom to be my own person and
develop my own opinions. And
please, oh please, show me that
you love me for "Love is the
Food of Life".

PAMELA LEGG, GR. 9, BRANDON, MAN.

Nozomi Aita, 10, Calgary, Alta.

I would make a recipe of good things to make the world a better place to live.

200 ml of Peace
2 table sp. of Love
5 tea sp. of Care
a pinch of Sharing
½ a pound of Happiness
1 ton of good and healthy food.

Bring five people into your home and give one Peace, one Love, one Care, one Sharing, and one Happiness to each one. Then tell the five people to share their Peace, Love, Care, Sharing, and Happiness. And for their friends to share with friends and so on until there is no one left to share with.

   With the ton of good and health food share it the same way as the Peace, Love, Care, Sharing, and Happiness.

Melanie Doerig, 11, Truro, N.S.

The world now is such a bore.
If I could make it there would be
   a lot more.
I would throw away all the bad
   bugs and bees
And have no such things as
   green peas.

Instead of snow falling from the
   sky
It would be mony falling high,
   high, high
There would be school (of course)
   but only for half a day.
Christmas would be longer, until
   the month of May.

Julie Mitchell, 11, Fredericton, N.B.

All that the world really needs is love, peace, and care.

Christine D. Marior, 10½,
Tsawwassen, B.C.

*In the world I'd plant lots of
    flowers,
In the houses the buildings and the
    towers,
The flowers would be up to every-
    one's knees,
The people would be happy and so
    would the bees.
This story can't be true although it
    sounds real great.
Because life can't all be a Rose
Bowl parade.*

Edward Gatt, Willowdale, Ont.

Pour faire un monde plus heureux
il faudrait partager nos biens
avec nos frères du tiers-monde.

Et bien sûr, il faudrait éliminer
la guerre mais, avant tout, il
faudrait faire la paix dan les
maisons.

   Mettez toutes ces choses
en pratique et vous serez
certainement heureux

Isabelle Fiset, St-Basile Le grand, Que.

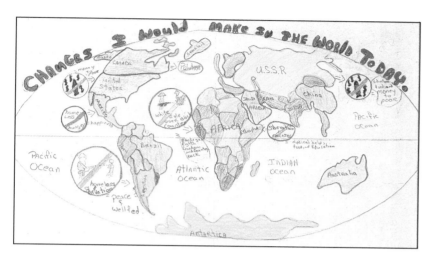

Janet Quitana, Gr. 8, Medicine Hat,
Alta.

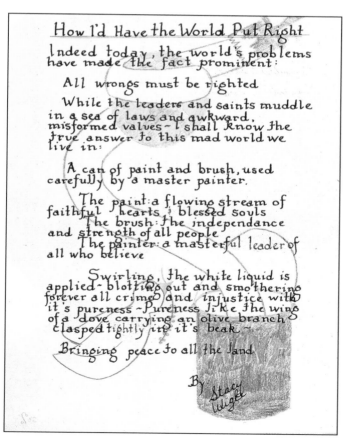

Stacey Wigle, Gr. 7, Kingsville, Ont.

71

SONYA DROUMTSEKAS, WATERLOO, ONT.

As I look amongst the shadows
   of our warped planet,
I find many inter-related flaws:
Unearthly crime and torture,
Black death,
Ever-spreading diseases,
Fatal drugs,
Extinction and endangering of
   now, helpless animals,
Famine,
Endless pollution,
Poverty,
Unfair prejudism,
And war.
A temporary peace surrounds
   our lives.
Unfortunately, in the adult world
   today,
A mere twelve year old child,
Could not set our world of
   darkness,
Free of these hazardous faults.
But if one could,
It would be
With the magical golden dust,
Of a good-natured fairy.

Pam Robinson, Gr. 7, Kingsville, Ont.

I would improve communication between all countries. . . .
Once I have made communication, and got them to understand each others problems,
peace would come. Trust, friendship and love for one another
would follow.

Susan Deforest, 11, Whitehorse, Yukon

Kristin Kan, Gr. 6, Nanaimo, B.C.

When I was little I thought my
   world was really great
Because I never ventured from
   my yard,
Never wandered through the
   streets.
But now I am older.
I see the world in which I live.
What I see is a struggling world,
A struggling human race.
If I could change the world,
I'd take away the crime and hate
And fill the world with love.

Melanie Vanstone, 11, Morden, Man.

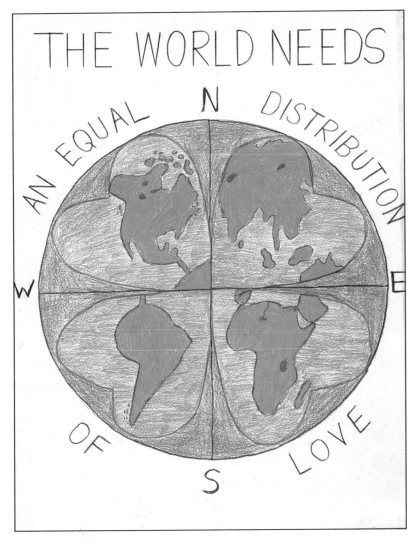

THE WORLD NEEDS AN EQUAL DISTRIBUTION OF LOVE

N W E S

ANDREW DEXTER, 11, FORT SMITH, N.W.T.

WORLD PEACE

Hope Peace Harmony Love Caring Sharing

TREVOR DAIGLE, 12, DUNCAN, B.C.

If I could change the world I would put the values of **Love**, **Freedom** and **Friendship** before anything else.

If I were to sing loud enough,
Would the people hear me?
If I were to write a tale,
Would the people know me?
If I were to build a tower,
Would they respect me?
If I were to become a flower,
Would they love me?

I sing, the people ignore me,
I write a tale, they don't believe
  me,
I build a tower, they draw mock-
  ing graffitti,
I become a flower, they step
upon me.

I shall be a politician,
The people will hear me.
I shall become a king,
The people will know me.
I will be a hero,
The people will respect me.
I will make much money,
The people will love me.

A politician is soon forgotten,
My song of **Love** will live forever.
A king's story is lost in time,
My tale of **Friendship** will be
  forgotten never.
Heroes die by thousands,
My tower is **Freedom**, forever to
  stand.
Gold is buried and forgotten,
While flowers spread across the
  land.

MARY MAVOURNEEN BURKE, 15, GLEICHEN, ALTA.

Dear World.......

Dear World, Why?

WHY DOES THERE HAVE TO BE POVERTY, FAMINE AND STARVATION? IF I COULD CHANGE THE WORLD, I WOULD LIKE TO HELP THE 3rd WORLD COUNTRYS, AND I WOULD HELP PEACE LIVE. I WOULD HELP IN ANY WAY I COULD TO STOP THE EXTINCTION OF ANIMALS. I WOULD JUST LIKE TO GIVE THE WORLD EVERYTHING I CAN, THAT WOULD HELP.

DAMIEN PHILLIPS, 10, OSHAWA, ONT.

They do not want crying. They want to be laughing now. please listen to us!

JASON HEATH, GR. 5, SELDOM, FOGO ISLAND, NFLD.

Our world is full of hunger, fear, pain, and hardship. Every headline of every newspaper brings reports of war, death, and misery. If we lived life through those newspapers, taking time to understand each emotion of the people connected with the depressing events, life itself would be worthless.

The one thing that can change all that, is love. Love for each other. The strength of love is so all-powerful, I believe that all problems can be defeated. That love is in work right now with projects such as Band Aid, Live Aid, Hear 'N Aid, Farm Aid, Northern Lights, USA for Africa, and Hands Across America. Each group is devoted to helping someone else, somewhere else, out. If we applied that type of energy, with that type of urgency, to each of the world's problems, we could overcome them all.

DEANNA BREITHAUPT, GR. 7, KINGSVILLE, ONT.

MISTY-LEE HEATHER, 12, MEDICINE HAT, ALTA.

In Charge For A Day. I would make a day where everybody has to be sad and do things we don't want to so we can appreciate being happy the rest of the year.

JENNY FLINT, GR. 3, WINNIPEG, MAN.

HOW I WOULD PUT THE WORLD RIGHT

FOOD TRUTH Future DREAM

UNION World mankind forever. smile people

Tomorrow AMERICA society Love

RUSSIA freedom GOD

HONESTY PEACE FRIENDS

MICHELLE BYCZKO, GR. 7, MIDLAND, ONT.

Dear World,
    How I'd put the World Right.
    I would have all parents hug and kiss their kids
while tucking them into bed at night. Then all the
boys and girls would grow up with love in their hearts
instead of hate and this would bring about peace
all over the world cause children don't like to fight.

                                    Love,
                                    Lisa Green

P.S. I still love being tucked
    in my bed at night.

LISA MARIE GREEN, 12, LABRADOR CITY,
NFLD.

**I'd put people of all different
colors in every family so they
would all grow up and know
each other better.**

DAWN MICHELLE BEATON, 7, MILL CREEK,
NOVA SCOTIA

If I could change the world today,
I'd make all things go my way.
No more crime or nuclear war;
No more pollution by the shore.
I'd preserve the forests and the
    lakes,
And save the wildlife God creates.
And one more thing that I would
    ask,
Which will never be an easy task;
Is to give the rain to other lands
And give a bigger helping hand.
I know it's not all up to me,
To build the world we want to see.
It's a world we want to know so
    well;
To live in peace and forever dwell.
Each one of us must do our part,
*Reach out and touch with an open
    heart.*
If everyone, my world could see,
Our world would live in harmony.

MICHELLE RAYLENE ALBRECHT, 12,
LETHBRIDGE, ALTA.

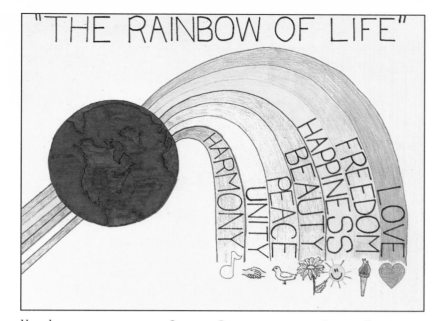

"THE RAINBOW OF LIFE"

LOVE
FREEDOM
HAPPINESS
BEAUTY
PEACE
UNITY
HARMONY

HEIDI LAUCKNER, 14 · SWARNALY BANERJEE, 14 · JENNIFER DONNELLY, 14

I'd have a Peace Day. On Peace Day you'd have to nod and say "Peace" to a stranger. When you meet a friend you should stop and have a chat. When you meet a relative, you'd have to hug or kiss them. Then at a certain time of the day, everyone would have to join hands and sing a song.

KATHLEEN HOGAN, 10, ST. JOHN'S, NFLD.

If I were God—or Allah,
I would change the world
By putting on a production, a
     play.
Gorbacev would be Reagan,
And Reagan would be
     Gorbachev;
Each representing their foe.
Botha would be black,
Terrorists would be passengers.
The Hungry would be nurtured;
The rich—starve . . .
Then, one glittering morning
A bomb will drop,
Descending slowly
Until it stops.
This climax stuns the onlookers.
It makes:
Gorbachev, Gorbachev.
Reagan, Reagan.
Botha, Botha.
Terrorists, Terrorists.
The Hungry, the Hungry.
Then the actors vanish behind
     the falling curtain.
Remembering their experience
     of being another,
Maybe we'll be treated as sister
     and brother.

CHRISTINE PIVETTA, 16, MONTREAL, QUE.

Peace
     Over
          War.

Wars are destructions that last for years,
Leaving peoples' hearts with many untold fears.
The fighting brings the young, old, and helpless to their knees,
While people turn deaf ears to their urgent pleas.

In these countries there should only be peace, no war,
Thus letting the needy peoples' spirits soar.
So hopefully they will forget their differences and find,
That peace and love will come to all mankind.

PEACE AND LOVE ON EARTH

Dear World, How I Would Put It Right.

I would put it right by stopping wars and making peace for all Third World Countries.

By Tammi Mannering.

TAMMY MANNERING, DELTA, B.C.

A Poem for the World

No more wars

Treat others with love.

Be respectful to others and fulfill our responsibilities.

Be kind love one another as they would love you.

Do deeds for others.

KERRI BROOKES, 9, TSAWWASSEN, B.C.

Dear World, How I would put the world right

I would make the world happy so no-one was sad.

SHERI HETTIG, GR. 5, WINNIPEG, MAN.

Dear Adinda,

It's really nice over here in Canada. There are many open fields, and meadows and plenty of forests for us to go walking in. There's even a place near by where we can go fishing.

Another good thing about Canada, is that you are free to give your own opinion without getting killed. Also when you grow up you can be whatever you want to be. I don't know if you'll like Canada, but I think it's a great place to live in.

Your good friend,
Jennifer

JENNIFER LORIA, 12, LONDON, ONT.

If I could make this world right I wouldn't change my life because God made my life just right for me. I would make all good dreams come true. Everyone would have the ability to become very successful.

JENNIFER POUW, 11

A flower is alive,
The petals are the soul,
Swirls of blue and green,
like an island in the blue water.

A lone flower peeking through the cracked, parched earth.
As the petals drop
The soul goes with them.

I dream of reviving the flower.
To bring it back to life,
Water it, feed it,
Give it a chance to bloom again.

NATASHA SLADEN, 11, HALIFAX, N.S.

I would invite all the warring parties to Canada to show them that it is possible to live in harmony with each other. Catholics and Protestants don't blow up each other like they do in Northern Ireland, Moslems and Christians don't kill one another as they do in Lebanon, whites don't kill blacks as they do in South Africa, but live and work together to build a beautiful future for us in this country.

We are a big and strong country, but we don't aspire to conquer other nations' territories. We could, if we wished to, invade Miquelon Island, like Argentina tried to invade the Falkland Islands not so long ago. But we won't ever do anything like that because we are a peaceful nation and France is our friend.

So, I would ask Mr. Mulroney to extend an invitation to all those who hate and fight to come and visit us and learn to live in peace as Canadians do.

Winston V. Barta, 15, Outremont, Que.

I would continue using children as peace-makers between countries. If children in warring countries become friends, then they, the future leaders, will not fight against friends.

Suzanne Meade, 13, Markham, Ont.

Tanya Lynn Murphy, 11, Newcastle, N.B.

David Gibb, Gr. 6, Lethbridge, Alta.

Pour être heureux dans le
monde il faut s'entraider
alors:

Éliminons la guerre
et les armes nucléaires

Soyons généreux,
Aidons les malheureux

Les personnes qui sont
dans le besoin devraient
avoir aussi de grands soins

Nous sommes gâtés!
Alors nous sommes
capables de partager

Leila Faraj
12 ans

Soyons heureux!

Leila Faraj, St. Luc, P.Q.

If every brother loved his sister,
What a happy family that would be.

If every family respected its neighbour,
What a friendly community that would be.

If every community worked together,
What a prosperous city that would be.

If every city helped another,
What a strong country that would be.

If every country lived in peace,
What a great world that would be.

Laura Plant, 12, Toronto, Ont.

This world is not very perfect. Since I live in this world, I would like to add somethings to it. First I would make another world and put all the bad people their. Later I would then on earth destroy all weapons. After that I would clean air, water and land. Then I would make a machine and turn all the bad people into good. With a little help I would make a bridge from earth to the other world. So the earth won't be overcrowded. Soon after that I would make all the wars stop.

Bobby Woodlock, 11, Quebec

I woke up feeling great pain in my leg. I looked around to see how bad the plane crash was. I turned over, it was obvious that everyone else was dead. I tried to pull my leg out from under a piece of the plane, but it was trapped. I was flying from Canada to a southern African country. It was very hot, so hot that I passed out.

I woke up again with this little black kid pulling my arm. I asked him to help me get my leg out. He didn't seem to understand my language, but he must have because he soon came back with several big strong men. They managed to remove my leg from under the plane, and took me back to their village. There they gave me food and a little water. I told them my name and how I was on my way to their country to help with the building of a bridge so that the people would have a better access to a river. I told them that there had been others from my country who had been killed in the crash, and that there would be more people arriving to help with the project. Soon the others did arrive and with the people of the village, we began to build the bridge. It was great fun and we seemed to understand each other quite well and talked freely. When I had to go back to Canada, I had made some great friends — and now they had access to the fresh water they needed. On the flight home I thought about how we helped each other and I wished that everybody would help each other.

HEIDI LAUCKNER

KRISTA LYNN WORTHMAN, 10, BONAVISTA, NFLD.

DOUGLAS PENICK, 11, HALIFAX, N.S.

81

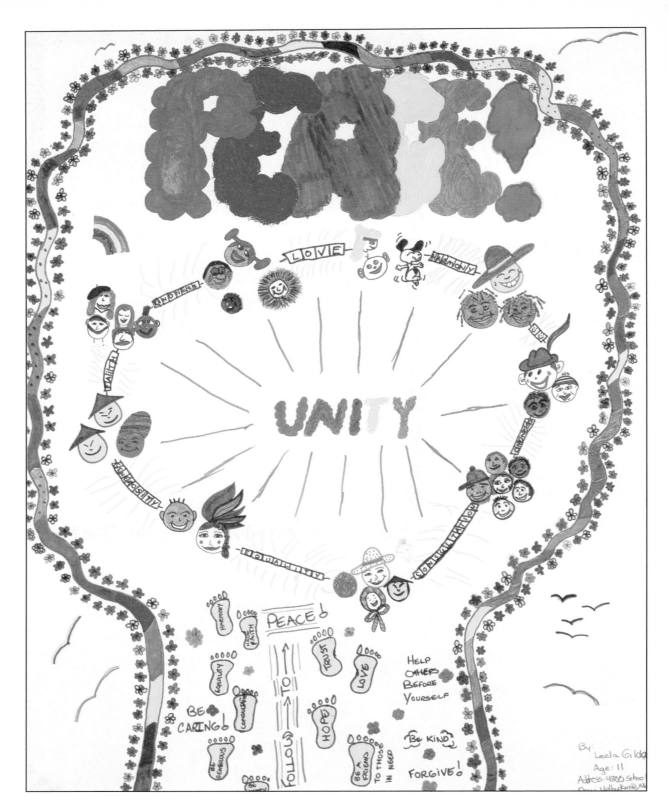

LEELA GILDAY, 11, YELLOWKNIFE, N.W.T.

When my dreams
Have come true,
Everything inside of me
Never will feel sorrow.

My mind sometimes
Yells at me, "Please

Don't refuse me," As the voice
Runs around in my head.
Everyday
A piece inside
Me, the
Sound does

Come to life.
Over & over I hear the crying of
Men looking for food for their
    family,
Eating sounds of greedy people,
As I

Try over again, I've
Really got to
Urgently help people
Everywhere.

LESLIE COUSINS, 10, FROBISHER BAY, N.W.T.

People would say hello,
To everyone they didn't know,
And those they knew,
They'd glance a smile,
They'd say come on let's chat a
    while.

Will there be a day,
When we could let the children
    play,
Alone on the streets at the end
    of the day?
We wouldn't worry if a stranger
    came,
And gave our child a ride to the
    game.

BRIDGITTE KINDERVATER, 12,
PRESCOTT, ONT.

DAVID ROONEY, 12, MONCTON, N.B.

HARRIET SHERRARD, 12, NEWCASTLE, N.B.

STACEY LEVINE, 10, BRANTFORD, ONT.

3 cups of love not sour nor sweet
Roll into balls on a mediator
    sheet.
Sprinkle some joy and a little
hope, have it blessed by the
kind hearted pope.
1 cup of flower, rose is the best.
Add some more for a hungry
    guest.
Skip the toxic waste, I'd prefer a
    natural taste!
Bake in the oven at 300 degrees
Yum! Smell the aroma in the
crisp cool breeze.
When the cake is baked and
ready to go it's so irresistable
you can't say "No!"
If only there was enough cake to
give to each child, lady and
man: to wars,
pollution, killing and crime we'd
put a ban.

AMY DMYTROW, 10

La plus belle chose c'est de vous aimer.

CHANTELLE DEON AND GISELLE DEYOUNG, 8,
PORT HAWKESBURY, N.S.

I'd make the world a better place by
King God to pass-out a law saying
that everybody had to help with
and World hunger

ROBBIE LANE, WILLOWDALE, ONT.

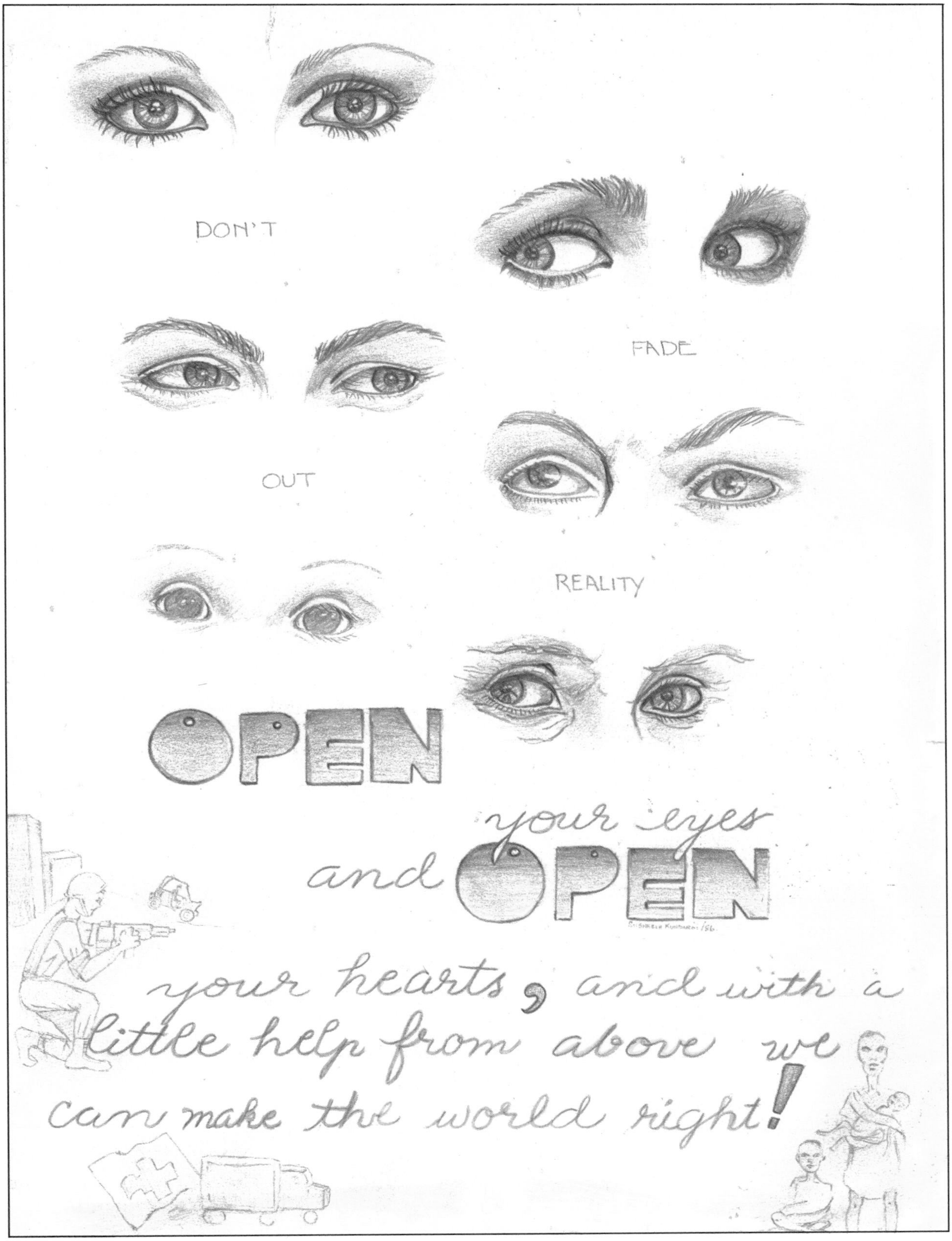

DON'T

FADE

OUT

REALITY

OPEN your eyes and OPEN

your hearts, and with a little help from above we can make the world right!

SUSHEELA KUNDARGI

MICHAEL SHIMIZU, 10, DUCHESS, ALTA.

JENNIFER LAINEY, 11, STEPHENVILLE, NFLD.

KELLY ONG, 14, NORTH YORK, ONT.

L-ove is important. Don't let it be destroyed by war and starvation.
O-ur plan is to help the poor and needy with God's word.
V-ictims of liquor suffer lots of accidents and trouble.
E-verybody should work together. One can't do it alone.

Put the first letters together and you have LOVE. Where there is love, there is peace. With love and peace you can share.

CURTIS KLEINSASSEN, 14, STE. AGATHE, MAN.

If I were to make the world happy I would make sure my family was not grumpy before they left for work or school. If my family went to school or work grumpily they might get others grumpy and then everybody would get everybody gumpy. This is why I never go to school grumpily, so everybody will be happy and peaceful. So everyday leave your house in a happy mood!

EMILY REDHEAD, 10, FORT SMITH, N.W.T.

Regardless of Religion and Culture, we are the same.

Shouldn't we care about others?

SARAH BARBER, 14

Dear World,

Nuclear war, poverty,
Starving people, discrimination.
Problems of the world Today,
I wish that they would all go away.

To make things better,
To bring the world to peace.
People should learn to trust each other,
To love everyone like a brother.

People should be more generous,
And help people less fortunate than themselves.
People should learn how to share,
To be concerned, and how to care.

All races of people,
All religions Too
Should teach people how to love, not how to fight,
Then the world would be alright!!!!!

LORI-ANN BUKSAK, 13, WINNIPEG, MAN.

If I could change the World by
Putting aside a day
With your neighbours once a
year. This day would be called
St. Neighbour Day!

A day of recognition
would be beautiful indeed.
a day of meeting people,
a day of fun and joy,
We'd all be out with happy
    thoughts;
Saying hi to one and all.
We'd sing, We'd laugh, We'd
    have a ball,
We'd shake, We'd bake till the
    end of night fall.
And never would we scream or
    shout,
for this would be based on joy.

EDDIE SHAKIN, 12, SCARBOROUGH, ONT.

I would try my best to make
peace all over the world, close
all the arms factories and the
money that would be spend in
arms would be used for research
in laboratories, so everybody
could have more chances to live
and play in peace. I also could
have a good talk to the rich
people, make them be less greedy,
and give some money to the poor
people in their country and poor
countries in the world. I would
beg them to put their money
into more good uses, such as great
jobs.

RICARDO DIAS, EMONTON, ALTA.

TAMARA-ANNE OROBKO, 11, WINNIPEG, MAN.

If I could change the world to make it a better place I would discover something so the horses wouldn't have to wear bearing reins and bits and bridles and to wear saddles on their backs. They wouldn't have to have tight strop around their tummy.

JENNIFER LITTLE, 9, LANSDOWNE, ONT.

I'd go to all the companies
And examine all machines.
Then replace the less required
With living human beings.

Then I'd lower welfare wages
And try to pay off debts.
Instead of making new ones
Off super-fast planes and jets.

LORRAINE PATON, 14, DUTTON, ONT.

There should be Cabbage Patch kids for $30 not $36.

AMANDA FRANCIS, 11, NANAIMO, B.C.

God of love, God of light, God of all power and might, how I would put the world right is to have a smile for everyday and for everyone to be merry and gay. Instead of bombs there would be songs and poems and tales and children playing with shovels and pails.

LISA ANN GREGORY, GR. 5, ST. JOHN'S, NFLD.

If I could rule the world for a day I would turn a leprechaun and jump on a rainbow.

LUC STEFANI, 5, VICTORIA, B.C.

I would make a law that if somebody didn't have enough money they could take the job of a rich person for a while. If I could put the world right it would be a miracle!

KRISTY WILLICK, GR. 5, NANAIMO, B.C.

Peace is very nice
But war is cold like a block of ice

AMY CIAMPICHINI, 11, QUICK, B.C.

I would make everybody equal and nobody would be better.

BETH KLASSEN

HEATHER CLEMENTS, 10, LYNDEN, ONT.

ANDREA MATTEATTI, 10, LETHBRIDGE, ALTA.

I would take the guns away and put the soldiers to work. I would bring all the kids with no moms or dad home with me.

DARCY BROWN, 10, SASK.

89

When is it going to End?
Let's talk .....
we can build hope.
Let's stop the violence,
it's just child's play
Let's talk .....
we might find we
share a common hope.

Done by: Angelo Curro
School: St. Margaret Mary
Grade: 8

ANGELO CURRO, GR. 8, WOODBRIDGE,
ONT.

I would write a book about how to keep peace. Then I would visit schools and teach the children not to fight. I'd teach them to be loving, generous, and if they have problems they should talk it over. I would teach them to say kind words like the prophet Zoroaster said—if you think pure thoughts it will lead to pure words and then it will lead to pure deeds.

NICOL SCOTT, 9, VERDUN, QUE.

I would give the poor people a whole year to be rich and a whole year for the rich people to be poor. There will be a lesson to learn and that lesson will be that everybody is a person and should be treated all the same because we all have feelings.

MIAFAYE SHELSTAD, 11, SEEBE, ALTA.

Africa is another country that's in need of help. If I would change Africa I would get rid of the prejudice and fighting and try to make it as wonderful and happy as I am.

ANGELA C. GARDIN, 9, LETHBRIDGE, ALTA.

Let's shoot for peace

ANGUS ROBINSON, 7

I'd rid the world of nuclear waste
Take it away, keep it away
Send it into outer space
Destroy it with a laser ray.

Poverty would be the next step,
Rich countries would give some
    money
Shelters would be well kept
Foods such as milk, meat and
    honey.

Star Wars I would demolish
Nuclear wars would be put aside,
Criminals I would punish
Make it known world wide.

Peace would overcome the world
Torture and execution I will
    destroy,
Nothing more cruel
And that would be my world
    change ploy!

CRAIG SILLIKER, 10, SUNNY CORNER, N.B.

A Better Place

Somebody once told me,
That no-one could change the
    world by himself.
But imagine a person,
Who always greeted you with a
    smile,
And,
A compliment.
Quite soon, it would catch on,
And you would welcome some-
    one
With the same kind smile.
A few words in praise, encour-
    agement, or thanks
Can make the greatest difference.
So the next time you see some-
    one,
Whether they be an acquain-
    tance or not,
Give them a marvelously friendly
    smile.
And remember,
One person alone CAN make
    the world a better place.

SARAH BARBER, 14, PARRY SOUND, ONT.

I WOULD FEED
THE WORLD
WITH
LOVE

MELISSA MCMAHON, 13, VICTORIA, B.C.

91

The good thing about our world is kindness.
The bad thing about our world is cruelty.
The good thing about our world is love.
The bad thing about our world is hatred.
The good thing about our world is peace.
The bad thing about our world is war.
The good thing about our world is health.
The bad thing about our world is sickness.
The good thing about our world is sharing.
The bad thing about our world is greed.
The good thing about our world is happiness.
The bad thing about our world is sadness.
The good thing about our world is comfort.
The bad thing about our world is poverty.

The good thing about our world is generosity.
The bad thing about our world is selfishness.
The good thing about our world is beauty.
The bad thing about our world is ugliness.
The good thing about our world is honesty.
The bad thing about our world is dishonesty.
The good thing about our world is friendship.
The bad thing about our world is enemies.
The good thing about our world is education.
The bad thing about our world is ignorance.
But the best thing about our world is —
People everywhere sharing and caring!

If we only had the power
We'd make the world like a
fresh spring flower
We'd keep the good things, and
throw out the bad,
So our world would be happy
and not so sad.
Cheerful, peaceful, kind, and
bright;
Then our world would be just
right!

GRADE 4 CLASS, MILL CREEK ELEMENTARY
SCHOOL, N.S.

**I would make some peace pills
and give them to the Presidents
of all Countries.**

VANESSA CHUNYS, 9, AGASSIZ, B.C.

JULIE COVELLI, 11, MISSISSAUGA, ONT.

Panel text:
- THE WORLD NEEDS CHANGING, THERE ISN'T ANY DOUBT
- ...NEEDS HELP IN LIBYA'S WARS. AND ALSO AFRICA'S DROUGHT
- IF I COULD HAVE MY SAY IN LIFE, I'D TRY TO KNOCK IT OUT / WORLD PEACE
- THE WORLD NEEDS CHANGING, TO THAT, WE ALL AGREE
- TO PUT AN END TO ARGUMENTS SO THAT WE ALL COULD BE / OW!
- FRIENDS WITH ONE ANOTHER FOR ALL THE WORLD TO SEE / HANDS ACROSS AMERICA!!
- THE WORLD NEEDS CHANGING, TO MAKE A BETTER DAY
- 'CAUSE NOW YOU CAN'T GO ANYWHERE TO HAVE A HOLIDAY / HOTEL / TOURIST / (THE BLOWING UP OF A TOURIST PLANE)
- IF WE PUT AN END TO FIGHTING, I'M SURE WE'D FIND A WAY.

CARLA EDWARDS, 13, GRAND FALLS, NFLD.

The world would be a better place,
If only people tried.
To help and serve and please
    others,
And let love be their guide.

If you can love your relatives,
Your friends and neighbors too,
The little wars that do go on,
Might stop inside of you.

And as each little war is stopped,
The big ones can be too,
Like waves that form when pebbles
    drop,
The peace that spreads from you.

We as the world can do something,
If only we would try,
To stop hunger, fear and pain,
Let's not have others die.

RACHEL ROTH, 11, MOUNT ALBERT, ONT.

I am as important to my small
environment as the sudden gust
of wind that fills the sails of a
stranded boat. But to the world
around me, I'm just a meaning-
less ripple in the sea of life. I
choose to describe how I live as
"One for all and all for one."
So I depend on others and others
can depend on me. I think if
more people believed in this,
then the world or a small part of
it would be a better place to live.

JANE SAWYER, 12, VANCOUVER, B.C.

Hunger	Hope
Oppression	Opportunity
War	Worth
Waste	Integrity
Overkill	
Uselessness	World
Lies	Optimism
Disease	Unity
	Love
Isolation	Disarmament
Crime	Co-operation
Hatred	Health
Apartheid	Affinity
Nuclear	Nurture
Greed	Generosity
Evil	Equality
Yoke	Youth
Oblivion	Ours
Underworld	Utopia
?	!

LARISSA PERGAT, 15, MONTREAL, QUE.

MATTHEW WESTENDORP, 11

We must find people who put others first. We must come up with a plan than can and will be carried on for generations. It is not what I or anyone else can do; it is what we all must work together for as one people instead of four and a half billion individuals.

CAROLYN CALWELL, GR. 8

Peace
Like dawn creeping
Slowly over the world
Banishing the cold darkness
Of the night
Comes slowly
Draining hatred
From our world.

Peace
Cannot come in a minute
It comes in small things
A smile, a truce
A friend
A kind word said
A wall between foes
Broken down.

Peace
Silver wings
That allow us to fly into a
Golden sky
Like a forgotten pearl
In an old marine oyster
Beneath the shimmering
Ocean waters.

Peace
An emotion reborn
A flower
In a dingy slum
Food for the hungry
No more cries
Time and love
Peace.

LAURA PENNY, 11, SYDNEY, N.S.

MARY GRACE OCAMPO, 10, SMITHS FALLS, ONT.

The world would be better if all the contries would get together. So nobody would fight And it would rain in africa. And if somme of the white man would stop treating black peopole like animals.

Tasha Riley, Gr. 6, London, Ont.

War
deadly murderous
fighting shooting killing
friendship amity concord tranquillity
loving caring understanding
silent still
Peace

Jason Perrino, Rankin Inlet, N.W.T.